Music in Worship

A NEW EXAMINATION OF AN OLD ISSUE

Music in Worship

A NEW EXAMINATION OF AN OLD ISSUE

Thomas C. Alexander

Gospel Advocate Company
Nashville, Tennessee

Copyright © 2010 by Gospel Advocate Co.

IT IS ILLEGAL AND UNETHICAL TO DUPLICATE COPYRIGHTED MATERIAL.

Scripture, unless otherwise noted, taken from the HOLY BIBLE, NEW INTERNATIONAL VERSION®. Copyright © 1973, 1978, 1984 by International Bible Society. Used by permission of Zondervan Publishing House. All rights reserved.

The "NIV" and "New International Version" trademarks are registered in the United States Patent and Trademark Office by International Bible Society. Use of either trademark requires the permission of International Bible Society.

All rights reserved. No part of this publication may be reproduced, stored in a retrieval system or transmitted in any form or by any means – electronic, mechanical, photocopy, recording, or any other – except for brief quotations in printed reviews, without the prior permission of the publisher.

Published by Gospel Advocate Co.
1006 Elm Hill Pike, Nashville, TN 37210
www.gospeladvocate.com

ISBN 10: 0-89225-572-2
ISBN 13: 978-0-89225-572-6

The praise of God which constitutes the community and its assemblies seeks to bind and commit and therefore to be expressed, to well up and be sung in concert. The Christian community sings. It is not a choral society. Its singing is not a concert. But from inner, material necessity it sings. Singing is the highest form of human expression. It is to such supreme expression that the vox humana *is devoted in the ministry of the Christian community.*

It is for this that it is liberated in this ministry. It is hard to see any compelling reason why it should have to be accompanied in this by an organ or harmonium.

– Karl Barth
Church Dogmatics, IV, 3, 866-67

Table of Contents

Introduction — 9

Chapter 1
Assessing the Old Testament Reasons — 19

Chapter 2
Evaluating the New Testament Reasons — 39

Chapter 3
Plumbing the Bottom Line — 59

Chapter 4
Psallo and Silence — 67

Conclusion — 81

Appendix 1
Atchley's Remarks Concerning the Use of *Psallo* in Literature Outside the New Testament — 87

Appendix 2
Instrumental Music and the Theology of Grace — 95

Appendix 3
Instrumental Music and Eternal Judgment — 101

Endnotes — 105

Introduction

Late in 2006, the Richland Hills Church of Christ in North Richland Hills, Texas (hereafter RH), announced that they would add a new worship service to their schedule. The service would be on Saturday evening and would have musical instruments. In addition, the Lord's Supper would be served. The plan was reported in various media outlets, and in February 2007 the service became a reality. To many people this was not particularly noteworthy. However, the move was significant for a congregation of churches of Christ who typically eat the Lord's Supper on Sunday and worship in song without instrumental accompaniment.

The rationale for and defense of the initiative was given by RH's preacher, Rick Atchley, in three lessons titled "The Both/And Church" that were made available to the public on RH's website and by recordings. As the title suggests, as far as music is concerned, Atchley contends that the church should not offer exclusively a cappella music as worship but should offer both a cappella and instrumental music. He identifies three factors that led to the RH action.

• The first is RH's need for more space for their weekly worship assemblies. Earlier efforts to schedule a third Sunday service were so disruptive that they proved unsuccessful. The Saturday meeting would accommodate members who prefer an instrumental service, thus freeing up needed space on Sunday at the traditional a cappella assemblies. According to Atchley's original explanation, the two worship services on Sunday would remain exclusively a cappella. Later, with apologies to the congregation, he said he had not intended to leave the impression that there would never be a Sunday instrumental service. In August 2007, Atchley announced that in addition to the Saturday assembly RH would have one a cappella Sunday service and one instrumental Sunday service.

• The second reason for adding instrumental music is related to mission. More people need to be reached with the gospel. The traditional posture of churches of Christ in insisting on exclusively a cappella worship is, in Atchley's mind, an unnecessary barrier to many who wish to come to Christ. Providing instrumental services will allow RH to reach more people.

• And third, the instrumental services will keep many dedicated and talented people from leaving RH in search of a church that gives them an instrumental option. Atchley says RH has "already lost way too many over a question that is way too unimportant."

The Main Issue

For whatever value these three reasons are for the RH church, Atchley admits that they are not the most important issue. He points out that there is a factor more fundamental than any of these. He says there are "two questions that have to get answered." First, "Is it biblically acceptable to worship God with instruments?" And second, "Even if it is biblically appropriate, is it right (or a good mission strategy) for this church at this time?" My evaluation focuses on the first of these questions for the following reasons.

• First, it establishes an initial point of agreement with brother Atchley. Until this first question is answered correctly, the other issues are beside the point. Only if instruments are biblically justified for Christian worship should a church consider how to use them, whether as a means of providing more space for worshipers, as a mission strategy, or as a way to keep people from leaving the congregation.

This is the question that Atchley says he will "tackle head on" in the second of his lessons – a lesson in which he says his task is "to make a case for why we should add instrumental music to our worship options." All three of his lessons are punctuated with affirmations of his commitment to be biblical. He suggests that the traditional perspective of churches of Christ that only a cappella praise should be offered in the church is a position "we're not defending biblically." [1] At the end of his series when he reviews what he has taught, he says, "We've tried to establish, and I believe we have, that it is biblical to praise God with or without musical instruments." Such language surfaces the question that must be raised in this study. Has he, in fact, biblically established his case for instrumental Christian worship?

• Second, Atchley and the RH elders have invited people to give a fair hearing to and an evaluation of what he says. Atchley's arguments have convinced the RH elders to endorse unanimously the decision to add the instrumental services. They have placed his arguments in the public arena and have suggested that the least people can do, in the words of a former RH elder, is "to study with an open heart the Word of God and make sure our conviction is based on that Word and not upon the tradition of men." So this present evaluation is not an invasion of anyone's private opinions or convictions. It is merely a response to the request that the RH church has issued publicly.

• Third, Atchley makes his case not only for the RH church but also in the apparent hope that he can influence other congregations. He says the lessons would be put on DVD so RH members could share them with anyone. Such a move is designed to be above board and to inform people of what RH is doing. But more seems to be implied. Despite the fact that Atchley says he is not trying to persuade people who prefer a cappella praise to worship any other way if that is their choice, he says that "someone has to be a leader" in advancing the ideas he proposes. The implication of his language is that he and the RH church believe they can provide the leadership. In fact, Atchley thinks that by becoming a "both/and church" RH "could inspire many other churches of Christ to be courageous in their kingdom efforts." It is difficult to resist the conclusion that brother Atchley hopes he can convince people in churches of Christ that it is right to worship with instruments and that congregations should make the option available to their members.

In November 2003, *The Christian Chronicle* reported that five urban congregations of churches of Christ had added instrumental services since the spring of 2001. The *Chronicle* identified the Oak Hills church in San Antonio, Texas, the Northwest church in Seattle, Wash., the Amarillo South congregation in Amarillo, Texas, the church in Farmers Branch, Texas, and the Southlake Boulevard congregation in the Dallas/Fort Worth, Texas, area. In December 2006, the *Chronicle* reported RH's plans for their instrumental service and said that of the congregations that have moved in these directions, "Richland Hills is, by far, the largest and most influential congregation to do so."

Since that time, Atchley's lessons have had an influence beyond the RH congregation. In January 2008, the Quail Springs church in Oklahoma City added an instrumental Sunday morning service. In a sermon delivered on April 8, 2007, seeking to justify the addition, the Quail Springs preacher, Mark Henderson, acknowledged that much of his lesson would overlap Atchley's lesson on biblical reasons for instrumental music. He praised Atchley and recommended that Quail Springs members listen to Atchley's lessons. He said the Quail Springs church "will join Richland Hills and others in becoming a both/and church." [2]

Reports of Atchley's lessons being recommended abound and links to them as resource materials are appearing on congregational websites. The First Colony church in Sugarland, Texas, made copies of Atchley's lessons available in quantity to the congregation, and Ronnie Norman, First Colony's preacher, encouraged members to listen to the lessons as the congregation's leadership considered whether to add an instrumental service. First Colony subsequently added a Sunday morning instrumental service.[3] No doubt other individuals and congregations have encountered or will encounter Atchley's arguments. We owe it to ourselves to evaluate them.

• This brings me to a fourth reason for evaluating brother Atchley's presentation. As one reads or listens to the spokesmen of the congregations of churches of Christ that have added instrumental worship, he will quickly recognize a similarity in argumentation.[4] Brother Atchley's presentation of the position appears to be the one that has received the most attention, perhaps because he represents, to use the words of *The Christian Chronicle*, "the largest and most influential congregation" to add an instrumental service. In addition, Atchley's efforts to promote unity between non-instrumental churches of Christ and instrumental Christian churches are widely known.[5] Consequently, by evaluating Atchley's arguments, one is able to evaluate the basic approach the new advocates of instrumental music within churches of Christ appear to be taking. Atchley's presentation reflects continuity with proponents who have immediately gone before him, and those who have come after him appeal to his argumentation.

In addition to allowing one to evaluate the current trend, this strategy also permits one to evaluate the arguments for instrumental music in Christian worship that have been made for more than a century. Recent advocates suggest that people should read old texts in fresh, new ways. They propose that their fresh, new reading of biblical texts points to the justification for instruments in church worship. Ironically, their reading of the relevant biblical texts is not new. The arguments made by brother Atchley and his fellow proponents are the arguments that have been made since the late 1800s among advocates of instrumental music.[6]

In 1948, G.C. Brewer evaluated some tracts that had recently been published in the advocacy of instrumental Christian worship. In pointing out that those tracts did not offer any new evidence, Brewer observed, "It is true that all that can be said on the subject, pro or con, is in print already. Books and debates on the question were written and published a generation ago."[7] In 2006, Everett Ferguson voiced a similar view when he wrote, "No new arguments have been advanced in favor of instrumental worship in the assembly. In that regard, the case is where it stood 100 years ago. The facts have not changed; attitudes have."[8] Pressing this point a little further, Jack Lewis has observed:

> There are no new arguments to present on the music question; the ground has been thoroughly plowed and replowed without convincing most instrumentalists. However, here as elsewhere in life there is always a new king arising who does not know Joseph [Acts 7:17-19]. This fact keeps us redoing what we have done many times before. In my opinion we now have a generation who do not know the lessons of the past. They need to be taught the issues on the music question.[9]

So I invite you to join me in what, I trust, will be a fair and honest evaluation of brother Atchley's effort to establish a biblical case for instrumental music as Christian worship.

Keeping the Main Issue in Focus

As I begin I should point out that my task in this study is not to present the positive case for non-instrumental Christian worship. This case has been argued substantially and persuasively by individuals within churches of Christ as well as by persons from other religious groups.[10] People who in the context of Christian faith and practice approach God musically by only singing are doing what Christians did in New Testament times and for centuries thereafter. Simply singing was the historical practice of the church for approximately 1,000 years of her existence.[11]

In fact, the practice of non-instrumental churches of Christ offering vocal music in worship is not in question. Brother Atchley acknowledges that it is right simply to sing in Christian worship. Concerning a cappella praise he says, "It is a wonderful, beautiful way to praise God. There is nothing wrong with that – never has been; never will be." He contends, however, that in addition to vocal praise the church should offer instrumental praise. So the burden of proof falls on his shoulders to demonstrate that the contemporary church should add to its worship a practice that was not in Christian worship in apostolic days. If churches of Christ should make a place for instrumental praise, then it must be shown that God approves instrumental worship for the church.

Atchley believes God does approve instrumental praise for the church. He believes it is biblical. He believes he has made sound biblical arguments that prove his case, and he invites others to evaluate his arguments. My purpose in this book is to determine whether the reading of biblical texts that brother Atchley proposes actually sustains his case for instrumental music as worship for the church.

Further, I must stress that the fundamental issue is whether the Bible justifies instrumental music for Christian worship and not some other issues that frequently intrude and contaminate the discussion. Sixty years ago G.C. Brewer had to keep the issue in focus as he evaluated the efforts of some brethren who were renewing the argument for instrumental worship. Brewer wrote:

We do not use instrumental music in worship because there is no authority for it in the New Testament. This is the position we take, and this is the issue between us and those who use the instruments. Anything else that may be brought into the discussion is irrelevant and confusing. This is the issue. It is not a question of who will be damned or who will not be damned. It is not a question of how good and sincere some people are who use instrumental music in the worship – good and sincere people by the millions sprinkle babies, confess to the priest, and count beads in prayer, etc. It is not a question of how far wrong a man may be and still be saved, or of how many things we may do that God does not authorize and still be Christians. *It is a question of what the New Testament authorizes us to do in worship and of what it does not authorize us to do.*[12]

Finally, the issue before us is not instrumental music per se, that is, instrumental music in and of itself. Christians who have contended exclusively for a cappella worship have often made it clear that they are not opposed to instrumental music per se. The issue at stake in this discussion is the use of instrumental music as a part of Christian worship. Do the biblical instructions that relate to Christian worship justify the use of musical instruments in the worship of the church? This is the question.[13]

Atchley's Positive Case for Instrumental Music

As pointed out earlier, Rick Atchley's arguments in support of instrumental music are not new. One finds the arguments scattered throughout the literature associated with this issue for more than 100 years. Whatever newness may be perceived in the present case is due to at least two factors. First, many people have never heard the arguments, either for or against instrumental music. The arguments are new to them, but, in fact, they are very old. And second, Atchley makes comments along the way that give the arguments an appearance of freshness. They come in his rhetorical packaging. Alan Highers has called attention to Atchley's skill in presenting his case. He observes that Atchley is "fluent, articulate, and clever" in making his arguments and that he is actually "more facile than his predecessors." However, he notes, "the arguments he makes have already been answered in the past." [14]

Atchley believes that most members of churches of Christ "in their hearts ... do not have a problem with instrumental music anymore. It's just that nobody has spoken to their heads." So he proposes "to speak to the heart and the head by going straight to the Word of God." [15] At the close of his first lesson he anticipates lesson two in which he will present his case for the instrument. He says, "Next Sunday we're going to open the Word of God, and we're going to stand under it and be blessed." Such language appears to mean that he will make, on the basis of Scripture, a rational argument (one that appeals to the head/mind) that supports the belief that he says most members of churches of Christ hold in the heart.

Not only does Atchley affirm his commitment to Scripture, but spokesmen for the RH church also acknowledge it. A former elder, in introductory comments to lesson two, says of Atchley, "I have never found his equal in his respect for the Word of God." A current elder, in an introduction to lesson one, says that Atchley is "a man who cares about the Bible and what it tells us. He never steps outside the authority of the Scriptures."

I am not calling into question brother Atchley's pledge of commitment to the authority of Scripture nor am I questioning the RH elders' appreciation of him for such a pledge. In fact, I commend them for the commitment. In an age when far too many people find seeking biblical reasons for faith and practice a burdensome irrelevance, Atchley and the RH leadership are on record saying it does matter what the Bible teaches. They want us to be sure our convictions rest on the Word of God.

Such a protestation is all the more reason to raise the question that drives this review, namely, "Has Atchley read Scripture properly and used it responsibly in making his case for instrumental music as Christian worship?" He thinks he has, and, apparently, the RH elders think he has because they have introduced instruments into their worship offerings on the basis of what Atchley has taught them. In introducing Atchley's lessons, a current RH elder says, "Since I am already aware [of] and familiar with what he's going to be teaching the next three weeks, I want you to know he has my full endorsement and the full endorsement of our full eldership as well." My task in this book is to determine whether Atchley's use of the biblical evidence in support of adding instruments to the church's worship deserves one's full endorsement.

Atchley makes his positive case for instrumental Christian worship in three stages. First, he gives his "Old Testament reasons" for accepting instrumental music. Second, he offers his "New Testament reasons" for accepting instrumental music. Third, he concludes his positive argument by considering what he calls the "bottom line" of the issue. I will evaluate each of these lines of argument in Chapters 1, 2 and 3 respectively. In Chapter 4, I will respond to brother Atchley's criticism of two arguments that have been made by a cappella advocates, arguments that relate to the Greek verb *psallo* and the silence of the New Testament on instrumental worship.[16]

Chapter 1

Assessing the Old Testament Reasons

Historically, people who have argued for instrumental music in church worship have made considerable use of material from the Old Testament. Brother Atchley is no exception. He turns to the Old Testament for his first line of argument.

Instrumental Music Commanded and Accepted by God in the Old Testament

Atchley's first two reasons are related, and I combine them in this first topic. His first reason is that God did not just allow instrumental music in the Old Testament, He commanded it. In the Old Testament instrumental music was not merely an aid to worship, it was worship offered in obedience to the command of God. The second reason is that in the Old Testament God was pleased with instrumental music offered from sincere hearts.

Atchley presents several Old Testament passages that support his claim (1 Chronicles 28:12, 19; 2 Chronicles 5:13; 7:6; 29:25-26; Psalms 33:1-3; 81:1-5; 92:1-3; 150; Exodus 15:20). These passages clearly show God's approval of instrumental praise in the Old Testament period. However, Atchley seems to have more in mind, and it is his apparent underlying agenda that raises questions.

Atchley's comments unfortunately leave the impression that Christians who oppose instrumental music for worship do not honor the Old Testament evidence that he has cited. After his lengthy review of the Old Testament texts cited above, Atchley says:

> With all of that as a background, I can't understand statements like I'm about to read. Last summer I spent three days in Abilene in the library reading everything I could read on this subject. I let every side have their best shot at me. I read debates that were one hundred years old. I read everything the anti-instrument position had produced. I came across this statement by one of their most virulent defenders. Regarding instrumental music in the Old Testament he wrote, "God tolerated it as he did David's polygamy and the rebellious kingdom, but he approved of neither." So the way he gets around the fact that there is instrumental praise all over the Old Testament is to say, "It's kind of like David's polygamy. God tolerated it but he hated it." I have to ask you, is that standing under the Word of God or over the Word of God? How on earth can you reach a conclusion that God was not pleased with what he ordered and commanded? In the Old Testament God didn't just allow instrumental praise, he ordered it.[1]

By saying he has read "everything the anti-instrument position has produced" and then quoting only one statement from such a vast body of information, Atchley leaves the impression that this view is representative of the position. He has identified a view that some a cappella advocates have embraced.[2] However, the view is not universal and does not represent the viewpoint of most current advocates for non-instrumental worship.

Atchley refers to Everett Ferguson's *A Cappella Music in the Public Worship of the Church* as "perhaps the best presentation of the anti-instrument position in the last century." If Ferguson is the best representative of the position, why doesn't Atchley mention Ferguson's view of Old Testament instrumental worship instead of, or at least in addition to, the opinion of the representative he quotes? Ferguson holds the same view regarding instrumental music in the Old Testament that Atchley does. Ferguson writes, "Instrumental music accompanied the sacrifices in the Old Testament, and that by divine authority. ... Instrumental music was itself an act of worship, and not just an aid, in the Old Testament."[3] Other published advocates of a cappella worship take this view as well.[4] And even the journal that Atchley read and from which he quotes one of the "most virulent defenders" of the anti-instrument position includes articles by non-instrumental brethren who affirm God's approval of instrumental praise in the Old Testament.[5]

Atchley often uses the expression "standing under the Word of God" to identify his posture regarding this issue. It is difficult not to recognize a contrast between the description of his own posture and the commentary on the one statement he quotes from the anti-instrumentalists – "I have to ask you, is that standing under the Word of God or over the Word of God?" It appears that Atchley is saying that in his advocacy for instrumental worship he honors the Word of God, he "stands under" the Word of God, but brothers who contend for exclusively a cappella worship do not honor the Word of God, but "stand over" it.

It is unfortunate that some who oppose instrumental music for Christian worship have resorted to questionable interpretations of the Old Testament evidence to argue the case. But it is equally unfortunate that by such "special pleading" brother Atchley prejudices the minds of his hearers against the non-instrumental view before he introduces any interpretation of biblical texts where there is any significant disagreement with most non-instrumental brothers and sisters.[6]

A cappella advocates have consistently contended that God's approval of instrumental music under the Old Covenant proves only that He sanctioned it under the Old Covenant. It does not provide independent authority for the practice in the church. This is true of both those who believe God only tolerated instrumental music under the Old Covenant and those who believe He commanded it.[7]

Individuals outside of churches of Christ have also recognized that one must look beyond Old Testament teaching to the New Testament for authority concerning music in Christian worship. This perspective is based on the truth that the Old Covenant God gave to Israel through Moses has been transcended by the New Covenant God has made with all humankind through Jesus Christ (Hebrews 1:1-2; 7:11–10:18). Edward Donnelly, a Reformed Presbyterian churchman, has written:

> The only possible scriptural basis for the use of instruments in worship is to be found in the Old Testament passages where the worshippers are described as using them or commanded to use them. ... But the overwhelming consensus of the church has been that these instruments were an integral part of the ceremonial worship fulfilled and abrogated in Christ. ... New Testament practice is against it.[8]

Atchley appears to be aware of this contention. Although he thinks people have made too much of the argument that instrumental worship was put away when the Old Covenant was transcended by the New, he makes no significant argument against the view. Nevertheless, he appears to react to it by strategically pushing Old Testament teaching regarding instruments into the New Testament. He seems to recognize that he cannot rest his case only on the Old Testament.

New Testament Commands to Sing Psalms

Atchley's first attempt to push the Old Testament perspective on instrumental music into the New Testament comes in a passing comment on Psalms 33, 92 and 150, all of which mention instruments. He says these Old Testament psalms are "the very psalms we are commanded in the New Testament to read and to sing." He questions, "Now doesn't it seem odd to you that the Holy Spirit would command us to sing psalms which we are forbidden to practice?"

Atchley does not elaborate on this point, but he leaves the impression that because Christians are commanded in the New Testament to sing psalms we should use the instruments mentioned in the Old Testament psalms.[9] He appears to be placing the singing of psalms by Christians on the same plane of command and obedience that is encountered in the Old Testament. Later in his lesson he makes remarks that imply that he views instrumental praise for Christians in the same way he views instrumental praise for the Old Testament Jews. Atchley says, "I do not believe God vacillates, liking one form of praise in one dispensation and disliking it in another."

I offer five observations concerning the argument based on the New Testament commands to sing psalms.

• First, Atchley involves himself in a self-contradiction with this argument. Later in his lesson he says, "New Testament commands to sing neither prescribe nor prohibit instruments." Now such a statement essentially makes void his appeal to the commands to sing the Old Testament psalms. If the New Testament does not prescribe instruments, as Atchley contends, then it does not command them, either explicitly by a direct statement or implicitly by references to psalms.

•Second, it is not at all certain that New Testament references to singing psalms refer directly to the Old Testament psalms. The consensus of current scholarship is that the words "psalm," "hymn" and "song" that appear in the New Testament (as in Ephesians 5:19; Colossians 3:16) are basically synonyms and fine distinctions of meaning cannot be made among them.[10] Only three New Testament passages provide explicit instruction concerning singing psalms (1 Corinthians 14:26; Ephesians 5:19; Colossians 3:16) and none points directly to Old Testament psalms.[11] These passages may have to do with songs of Christian origin.[12] If this is the case, Atchley's appeal to the singing of Old Testament psalms is not relevant. However, because these New Testament references might include Old Testament psalms, I will accept his understanding for the argument.

• Third, some problematic implications follow from Atchley's remarks about the Old Testament psalms. It is well documented that the church in New Testament times did not approach God with instrumental music.[13] Although Atchley cannot bring himself to say there were no instruments in New Testament churches, he concedes that on the basis of what we know about the church in New Testament times "the worship was almost exclusively a cappella."[14]

If a New Testament command to sing psalms means to sing the Old Testament psalms with the use of musical instruments, how does one reasonably explain the absence of such instruments from early Christian worship? Surely the inspired apostles understood the implications of God's commands, and the earliest Christians who "devoted themselves to the apostles' teaching" (Acts 2:42) would have been instructed in those commands. If Atchley's argument were valid, one would expect to find some evidence of the use of instruments by the apostles and the churches they established. However, there is no evidence of such.

Atchley explains the absence of instruments in terms of the early church's attempt to be sensitive to its culture. To worship without instruments was, in his words, "the culturally appropriate and missionally strategic thing to do to reach their culture." This is an assertion for which he offers no proof. Further, he does not explain how giving up the use of instruments would function as a mission strategy for the New Testament church in a culture in which instrumental music was prevalent. Atchley contends that the church should use instrumental music today because in our culture instrumental music is so prominent. It is difficult not to recognize a certain inconsistency in his argument. Ancient and modern cultures have recognized the value of instrumental music and have used it for both noble and ignoble purposes. How can it be that foregoing the instruments served a missionary function in the first century but using them serves a missionary function today? Or if the modern church can reach people better by using instruments, why could not the ancient church have reached people better by using them?

Atchley's argument taken at face value, however, only deepens the problem. Remember, he has argued that Christians are commanded to sing the Old Testament psalms and that psalms by definition entail instrumental music. It is difficult to imagine that the apostles who lived by the rule "We must obey God rather than men!" (Acts 5:29) would lay aside something God had commanded the church to practice in order to reach their culture. Paul the apostle sought to be sensitive to his culture in preaching the gospel. He said, "I have become all things to all men so that by all possible means I might save some" (1 Corinthians 9:22). However, Paul had his boundaries. In response to those who might question his instructions regarding a matter of church practice, Paul said, "If anybody thinks he is a prophet or spiritually gifted, let him acknowledge that what I am writing to you is the Lord's command. If he ignores this, he himself will be ignored" (14:37-38). It is unthinkable that Paul would have advised the church not to do something God had commanded her to practice in order to reach the culture.

• Fourth, not only does this argument call into question the actions of the apostles, but it also causes one to wonder about the practice at RH.

Atchley says, "You need to hear this loud and clear. There is no intention of this leadership to force anyone to worship any other way if that is their choice." RH members are given the choice of attending the a cappella service on Sunday or the instrumental service on Saturday or Sunday. This is puzzling since Atchley has affirmed with equal passion that instrumental music in the Old Testament worship was a matter of command and obedience, has suggested that Christians are commanded to sing psalms with instruments as was done in the Old Testament, and has contended that God's attitude toward instrumental music under the New Covenant is the same as it was under the Old Covenant.

If the model for the church's musical practice is the Old Testament, then on whose authority can RH give the church choices in how she is to approach God musically? If the use of instruments in the Old Testament was a matter of obedience to God's commands and God's perspective has not changed in the New Testament, as Atchley contends, then he cannot place their use in the both/and category. If instruments are included in God's commands for the church, they must be used. On the basis of Atchley's own argument, the a cappella-only Sunday service at RH would be in violation of God's commands because at that service people do not practice the psalms they are commanded to sing. Atchley's concession that Christians can choose to worship with instruments or without them essentially invalidates his argument that New Testament commands to sing psalms implies the use of instruments.

• Fifth, Psalms mentions several practices associated with Old Testament worship in addition to the use of instruments of music. Must Christians also implement these acts in our assemblies? Must we in our Christian assemblies sacrifice a freewill offering (Psalm 54:6), sacrifice thank offerings (50:14, 23), present sacrifices or burnt offerings (50:8; 66:13-15), make a festal procession up to the horns of the altar (118:27), and fulfill our vows in the temple courts in Jerusalem (116:18-19), all of which are included in Psalms? Must we practice the dance that Atchley reads over hurriedly and without comment in Psalm 149:3 and 150:4? Has the Holy Spirit commanded us to sing psalms we are forbidden to practice? Atchley has offered no interpretive strategy that will show why the instruments mentioned in the Old Testament psalms should be included in Christian worship but not the other acts.

John Price has correctly recognized the weakness of this argument. "If this is true, then everything else mentioned in the psalms must be brought into the church as well."[15]

All of this should cause one to recognize that the New Testament teaching regarding singing psalms constitutes no basis for using instruments in Christian worship.

Instruction for Instruments Given Before the Law

Atchley's second effort to push Old Testament teaching toward the New Testament is an appeal to Psalm 81:1-5 that mentions the tambourine, harp, lyre and ram's horn in a summons to celebrate an appointed feast. The writer of the psalm says, "this is a decree for Israel, an ordinance of the God of Jacob. He established it as a statute for Joseph when he went out against Egypt, where we heard a language we did not understand" (vv. 4-5).

Atchley contends that this psalm indicates that God commanded instrumental praise before he gave the law of Moses. He also notes that Miriam and the women sang and played tambourines before the law was given (Exodus 15:20). He suggests that this shows a weakness in the view that instrumental worship was made obsolete when the old Mosaic covenant was superseded by the new covenant of Christ. In his view, because God instructed Israel in instrumental music before the law was given, it should transcend to the New Covenant.[16]

Biblical scholars are uncertain concerning at least two exegetical issues presented by Psalm 81. The first is the exact time indicated by the expression "when he went out against Egypt" (v. 5). Does it refer chronologically to a time before Israel left Egypt, or is the language inclusive of the whole exodus period? The other issue is the identification of the feast referred to by the psalm. Is it Passover or the Feast of Tabernacles?[17] However, even if Psalm 81 refers to instruction God gave to Israel prior to the giving of the law, it does not justify instruments for the Christian assembly, as the following observations will show.

• First, if we follow Atchley's method, we must recognize that a number of Old Testament practices were introduced before the law was given that could be justified for Christian practice, such as animal sacrifices (Genesis 4:3-5; 8:20-21), keeping the Sabbath (Exodus

16:23-26), and the dancing of Miriam and the women (15:20) to name only three. Are we prepared to accept in church life these and all other practices that were introduced before the law? Atchley does not offer any assistance in helping us decide which of the practices we should accept and which ones we should not. He is certain we should use the instruments, but why not the others?

• Second, and a greater problem for individuals who make this argument, if Psalm 81 justifies the use of instruments in Christian worship, it should also justify the Christian observance of the feast mentioned there. Should the church observe the feast (whether Passover or Tabernacles) because the instructions for the feast were given before the law? Again, Atchley offers no help for answering this question.[18]

• Third, the instructions for the Feast of Tabernacles were given with the law (Leviticus 23:33-43; Numbers 29:12-39; Deuteronomy 16:13-17). They, consequently, were terminated for Christians with the fulfillment of the law in the New Covenant. And while the initial instructions concerning Passover were given before the law (Exodus 12:1ff), they were later incorporated into the law's instruction concerning Passover/Feast of Unleavened Bread (23:15; Leviticus 23:4-8; Numbers 28:16-25; Deuteronomy 16:1-8). Because the New Testament says that Christ is our Passover, it would appear that with His fulfillment of the law, the Passover was fulfilled as well (1 Corinthians 5:7; see also Colossians 2:16-17). Thus, the church does not observe Passover.

The fact is, all Psalm 81 contributes to this discussion is the awareness that instrumental music was associated with the feast in Israel to which it refers. Obviously God accepted the instruments in that context. However, the psalm has no relevance at all to the issue of instrumental music as an act of Christian worship.

Instrumental Music in the Church Anticipated by Messianic Prophecy

Atchley's most direct effort to get Old Testament ideas concerning instrumental music into the New Testament comes in what he states as his third Old Testament reason for using instruments, namely, messianic prophecy anticipated that instrumental music would continue in the coming kingdom. His argument is based on the quotations of two Old Testament texts in two New Testament documents.

The Old Testament Quotation in Hebrews 1:8-9

Atchley first appeals to the quotation of Psalm 45:6-7 in Hebrews 1:8-9 which reads as follows:

> Your throne, O God, will last for ever and ever, and righteousness will be the scepter of your kingdom. You have loved righteousness and hated wickedness; therefore God, your God, has set you above your companions by anointing you with the oil of joy.

He correctly explains that these verses are from a psalm whose original setting was the wedding of an Israelite king. He observes that the Holy Spirit guided the writer of Hebrews to apply these verses to the Messiah. If this were all Atchley said concerning these texts, one could hardly object because they are well-known truths. However, he makes other observations on these passages that raise concern.

Atchley argues his case, not on the basis of what the writer of Hebrews says, but on the basis of what he does not say. Atchley calls attention to Psalm 45:8 that immediately follows the passage cited in Hebrews 1 – "All your robes are fragrant with myrrh and aloes and cassia; from palaces adorned with ivory the music of the strings makes you glad." He then comments, "Certainly the people who knew that psalm well would not possibly imagine the Messiah was not pleased with instrumental praise." He makes no other comments about these passages. His remark is supposed to be sufficient evidence that this messianic prophecy anticipated the use of instruments of music in the church.[19]

One of the most difficult issues in biblical interpretation concerns how New Testament writers use the Old Testament, and the writer of Hebrews presents us with some of the most challenging aspects of the issue. The issue is complex and deserves more than sweeping generalizations.[20] However, in the present case, an elementary investigation of the relevant passages reveals a questionable handling of the biblical text by brother Atchley and the consequent fallacy of this aspect of his argument for instrumental Christian praise.

- First, it is unlikely that "the people who knew that psalm well," to use Atchley's own words, would have even been aware of a reference to "the music of the strings" in Psalm 45:8 [44:9 Grk.]. [21] It is recognized in biblical scholarship that the Old Testament text quoted in Hebrews is the text of the Greek Old Testament (Septuagint/LXX). James Thompson has noted, "The writer of Hebrews knows the Old Testament only in the Greek version." [22] More recently William Lane has pointed out, "a virtual consensus has been reached that the writer [of Hebrews] read his Bible in Greek." [23] Lane further observes that the social and religious background of the original readers of Hebrews may be traced to the Hellenistic synagogue where their source of authority was the Greek Old Testament. Lane says, "The writer is confident that he can win a hearing for what he wished to say by employing vocabulary sanctioned by the Greek Scriptures." [24] Carson, Moo and Morris underscore this view when they say, "Furthermore, the author cites the Greek Old Testament as if he assumes that his readers will recognize its authority." [25] At another place in his lesson, Atchley says that the Septuagint was the Bible of the early Christians.

It is important to note that no reference to "the music of the strings" is in Psalm 45:8 [44:9 Grk.] in the Septuagint. For an impression of how an early Christian audience familiar with the Old Testament in Greek would have known the passage, consider this quotation of Psalm 45:6-8 [44:7-9 Grk.] by Justin Martyr around A.D. 155-161.

> Thy throne, O God, is forever and ever; the scepter of Thy kingdom is a scepter of uprightness. Thou hast loved justice, and hated iniquity; therefore, God, Thy God, hath anointed Thee with the oil of gladness above Thy fellows. Myrrh and stacte and cassia perfume Thy garments, from the ivory houses, whereby they have made Thee glad.[26]

The *New English Translation of the Septuagint* that was published in 2007 renders Psalm 45:8 [44:9 Grk.] as follows: "Myrrh and myrrh oil and cassia waft from your clothes, from ivory bastions, with which they made you glad." There is no mention of "the music of the strings." The author and the original readers of Hebrews would not have thought to make an argument based on the "music of the strings" in Psalm 45:8

as brother Atchley does because that expression was not in the Old Testament they knew.

The allusion to the music of stringed instruments that appears in Psalm 45:8 [45:9 Heb.] in a number of English Bibles (ASV, NASB, RSV, NRSV, NEB, NIV) is based on a conjecture concerning the meaning of an ambiguous term in the Hebrew text of the psalm. Some scholars think that understanding the Hebrew word *mini* as a repetition of the word *min* that appears earlier in the verse creates an unnecessary redundancy. They prefer to understand *mini* as an abbreviation or a corruption of the plural *minim* that connotes stringed instruments, as in Psalm 150:4 where the full plural occurs.[27] Other scholars opt for alternative understandings of the difficult language.[28] One should be leery of basing an argument so squarely on an ambiguous text.

All this demonstrates that the certainty with which the writer and readers of Hebrews would have understood the Messiah's pleasure with instrumental praise from Psalm 45:8 that Atchley proposes is not certain at all.

• In the second place, even if Atchley's argument is taken at face value (that is, if we accept the translation "music of the strings" in Psalm 45:8), we can recognize its impropriety as a justification for instrumental music in church worship.

The writer of Hebrews did not expect all the language surrounding a given quotation from the Old Testament to be equally applicable in his messianic use of a text. This is evident from his use of 2 Samuel 7:14 in Hebrews 1:5, the same passage in which he quotes Psalm 45:6-7.[29] The language was originally spoken to David concerning God's relationship to Solomon. The Hebrews writer applies the first part of the verse to the relationship between God and Jesus His Son – "I will be his Father, and he will be my Son" (Hebrews 1:5). However, the last part of 2 Samuel 7:14, which the writer of Hebrews does not quote, says, "When he does wrong, I will punish him with the rod of men, with floggings inflicted by men."

If Atchley's method for interpreting Psalm 45 in Hebrews 1 is applied consistently, the last part of 2 Samuel 7:14 should be messianic. However, it is clear that the writer of Hebrews did not have this understanding. In Hebrews 4:15 the writer affirms that Jesus our high priest was without sin. It is obvious that the writer's use of 2 Samuel 7:14 in Hebrews 1:5 is limited to the point he is supporting by the part of the verse he quotes. The words that follow in the last part of 2 Samuel 7:14 have no messianic relevance. There is no reason to think Psalm 45:8, "the music of the strings makes you glad," would be any different.

Further, Atchley's reading of this text to support instrumental worship in the church is compromised by what we know about Jesus the Messiah. Being made glad by the music of the strings (Psalm 45:8) is only one aspect of the psalm's description of the king. What about these other matters? He would wear fragrant robes and live in palaces adorned with ivory (Psalm 45:8). He would have a wife and sons and a harem (v. 9). He would advance his cause by riding forth victoriously, using his sword and his arrows against his enemies (vv. 3-5). There is no evidence that any of these things was true of Jesus.[30] Just like these descriptions of the Israelite king, the remark about the king being pleased with the music of the strings (if indeed that is the way the verse should be translated) has no messianic relevance. The only part of Psalm 45 that has messianic relevance in Hebrews 1 is the section the Hebrews writer cites to bolster the point he is arguing – Jesus is superior to the angels.

Brother Atchely's argument for instrumental praise in the church from Psalm 45 is without merit.

The Old Testament Quotation in Romans 15:8-9

The second messianic prophecy that Atchley says anticipates instrumental praise in the church is the Old Testament passage cited by Paul in Romans 15:8-9.[31] In fact, Atchley says he finds this passage "even more convicting." In the text in question Paul writes:

> For I tell you that Christ has become a servant of the Jews on behalf of God's truth, to confirm the promises made to the patriarchs so that the Gentiles may glorify God for his mercy, as it is written: "Therefore I will praise you among the Gentiles; I will sing hymns to your name."

Atchley rightly points out that Paul appeals to the Old Testament in Romans 15:9. However, his remarks that follow are inaccurate and misleading.

• First, Atchley says there is a problem of knowing exactly which passage Paul is quoting since, he says, "there are several places in Psalms where there is a verse like this." He initially suggests the quotation is most likely from Psalm 18:49 or 57:9, but later he specifically says that Paul is quoting 57:7-9, and he places these verses on a projection screen for his audience to read.

There should be no problem of knowing which passage Paul is quoting and which one he is not quoting. He is quoting Psalm 18:49 or 2 Samuel 22:50. He is not quoting Psalm 57:9 as brother Atchley affirms. This can be confirmed by comparing the Greek text of Romans 15:9 with the respective Old Testament passages in the Greek Old Testament from which Paul is quoting. The words in Romans 15:9 are verbatim from Psalm 18:49 [17:50 Grk.] in the Greek Old Testament but with one exception – the omission of the vocative "O Lord." Paul's citation is verbatim from 2 Samuel 22:50 in the Greek Old Testament but with two exceptions – the omission of the vocative "O Lord" and the omission of the preposition *en* from the expression "to your name." The language quoted in Romans 15:9 is not the language of Psalm 57:9 [56:10 Grk.] that translates as follows: "I will confess (*exomologeo*) to you among the people, O Lord, I will sing (*psallo*) to you among the Gentiles" [trans. TCA].

Even if one is familiar with only the English text of the Bible, he can know the passage Paul is quoting. The footnote at Romans 15:9 in the New International Version from which Atchley routinely reads in his lessons identifies the quotation from 2 Samuel 22 or Psalm 18. There is no mention of Psalm 57. One can also find this information in the commentary literature on Romans 15 in which writers consistently note the passage Paul is quoting.[32]

Further, Atchley's remarks about *zamar*, a word that appears in the Hebrew text of the passage Paul quotes (Psalm 18:49 [18:50 Heb.]), are less than clear and leave an impression that is less than accurate. The word *zamar* is translated in the Septuagint with the Greek verb *psallo* that is rendered in major English translations of Romans 15:9 as "sing hymns" (NIV), "sing" (KJV, NASB) or "sing praises" (NRSV). Concerning *zamar* Atchley observes, "You won't find a lexicon anywhere that fails to include instruments in defining what the word *zamar* meant." He concludes, "So Paul says, 'Here's the prophecy that in the messianic age the Gentiles will *zamar* to your name.'"

Then Atchley says, "just to be sure what the word means, look at Psalm 57:7-9 *where Paul is quoting that verse*" [emphasis mine, TCA]. I will return to this erroneous appeal to Psalm 57 later. But first, I must call attention to Atchley's remark about lexicon definitions of *zamar*.

Atchley's statement concerning lexicon definitions of *zamar* does not accurately represent the facts. It fails to take into consideration the nature of information included in lexicons in general and obscures what the standard Hebrew lexicons actually say regarding *zamar* in particular.

A lexicon (or dictionary) gives the range of meanings a term can have based on the various ways that term is used in available literature. Frequently the etymology (root meaning and history) of a word is given. However, some uses of a term may have little or no connection with its root meaning, a fact that is widely recognized among interpreters of biblical and non-biblical literature. As Ferguson has correctly said, "Actual word usage and context determine word meanings in given passages, not etymology." [33]

Consequently, a lexicon will list a number of possible meanings (range of meanings) of a term along with biblical passages (and in some cases passages in related literature) where these meanings are understood on the basis of the various contexts in which the term is used. In light of the nature of such listings, one cannot take a single possible meaning of a term and assume that is the meaning every time the word occurs.[34] Atchley's observations about *zamar* do not demonstrate an awareness of these fundamental rules concerning the nature of word usage in the Bible and the proper use of a lexicon. His observation, "you will not find a lexicon anywhere that does not include instruments in defining what the word *zamar* meant," has the tone of affirming what the word always meant. It appears that Atchley is asserting that the lexicons indicate that when the word is used in the Old Testament it always includes the use of instruments. It is crucial to understand that this is not true.

The two most widely used Hebrew lexicons are the Brown, Driver and Briggs *Hebrew and English Lexicon of the Old Testament* and the Koehler and Baumgartner *Hebrew and Aramaic Lexicon of the*

Old Testament. Brown, Driver and Briggs give the basic meaning of *zamar* as "make music in praise of God." In this regard the lexicon specifies two uses of the term. The first use is to connote "singing." The lexicon cites approximately 40 instances of this use of the word. In some of these passages instruments are mentioned in the context suggesting that the singing was likely accompanied. However, in many of the cases the term is used without a reference to instruments in the context. BDB's second category of the word's use is "playing musical instruments," and six instances of this use are cited. The lexicon also cites two instances in which the term means "trim, prune." [35]

The Koehler and Baumgartner lexicon lists four categories of use of the term *zamar* – (1) to play an instrument, sing; (2) to praise; (3) to sing, praise; (4) to play an instrument. The lexicon also notes two passages where the meaning is "prune." [36]

So the lexicons identify the use of *zamar* in an instrumental setting in some Old Testament passages. However, by listing other uses of the word they make it clear that the playing of an instrument of music does not inhere in the word itself. That is, the word does not always mean to play on an instrument or to sing with the accompaniment of an instrument in its Old Testament occurrences. That the term sometimes appears in an instrumental context is certain. However, in many cases in the Old Testament, the word *zamar* means simply to sing or to praise.

The most determinative factor in recognizing the meaning of a word is the context in which it is used. In the case of *zamar* one should consider in each occurrence of the term whether the surrounding language suggests the presence of instruments. There is no reference to instruments in the context of the text that Paul quotes in Romans 15:9. And further, the language of the verse itself points to verbal praise. The Hebrew verb that stands in parallelism to *zamar* in Psalm 18:49 [18:50 Heb.] is *yadah*, which means "give thanks, laud, praise." [37]

More relevant to this discussion is the fact that in Romans 15:9 Paul is not quoting the Hebrew text at all but the Greek translation of the Old Testament. The Hebrew *zamar* is represented by the Greek verb *psallo*, a term that also had a variety of uses and which in Romans 15:9 and Psalm 18:49 [17:50 Grk.] stands parallel to the Greek verb *exomologeo,* "confess, praise." [38] In Paul's two other uses of *exomologeo,* he seems to have in mind a verbal act. Note his quotation of Isaiah 45:23 in Romans 14:11: " 'As surely as I live,' says the Lord, 'every knee will bow before me; every tongue will confess [*exomologeo*] to God,'" and his adaptation of the language in Philippians 2:11: "and every tongue confess [*exomologeo*] that Jesus Christ is Lord, to the glory of God the Father." No contextual evidence suggests that Romans 15:9 describes anything other than verbal praise of God.

If the meanings of *zamar* and *psallo* inherently involve playing instruments or singing with instrumental accompaniment, and these meanings were naturally understood by early Christians as Atchley suggests they were, one would expect to find some evidence of the use of instruments in the primitive church. However, the evidence of history is to the contrary. The absence of any evidence of instruments in early Christian worship is powerful testimony to the fact that the terms under consideration do not inherently involve the use of instruments. Wm. M. Green pointed out concerning the term *psallo*, "If the evidence points to the absence of instrumental music in the ancient church, the lexicographer should follow the evidence of history." [39]

It has been noted earlier in this book that historians acknowledge the absence of instruments from early Christian worship. James McKinnon has observed, based on his study of the relevant literature from the early church, that the Church Fathers were both uniform and vehement in their opposition to instruments.[40] The absence of any reference in the New Testament to instruments in church worship joins the vehemence and uniformity of the Church Fathers' polemic against instrumental music to confirm the non-instrumental understanding of the New Testament language. Whatever the range of meanings for the terms *zamar* and *psallo*, the earliest Christians understood them in a non-instrumental sense when applied to the church's worship.

At this point I return to Atchley's introduction of Psalm 57 into the argument. He places these verses on a projection screen for his audience to read and says, "just to be sure what the word means, look at Psalm 57:7-9 *where Paul is quoting that verse*" [emphasis mine, TCA].

> My heart is steadfast, O God, my heart is steadfast; I will sing and make music. Awake, my soul! Awake, harp and

lyre! I will awaken the dawn. I will praise you, O Lord, among the nations; I will sing of you among the peoples.

It is important to understand that this is a factual error. By erroneously saying Paul quotes Psalm 57:7-9 in Romans 15, Atchley leaves the false impression that Paul is quoting an Old Testament passage in which *zamar* (Heb.) and *psallo* (Grk.) appear along with a reference to instruments. Psalm 57 is a text that demonstrates that both terms are sometimes used in an instrumental context (note the mention of harp and lyre in verse 8). However, and this is the crucial point here, Paul does not quote Psalm 57:9 in Romans 15:9. He does quote Psalm 18:49, a verse in which *zamar* and its Greek equivalent *psallo* mean simply to sing or to praise. The argument that Atchley finds "even more convicting" for his case actually rests on a false premise. He bases his argument on a verse that Paul does not even quote.

And one other observation before I leave the argument that messianic prophecy anticipated instrumental music for the church. Deuteronomy 18:20-22 says:

> But a prophet who presumes to speak in my name anything I have not commanded him to say, or a prophet who speaks in the name of other gods, must be put to death. You may say to yourselves, "How can we know when a message has not been spoken by the LORD?" If what a prophet proclaims in the name of the LORD does not take place or come true, that is a message the LORD has not spoken. That prophet has spoken presumptuously. Do not be afraid of him.

If, as Atchley contends, the Old Testament prophets predicted instrumental music would be in the church, it is indeed strange that no evidence of it is in the apostolic church. Atchley says David predicted in Psalms 45:8 and 57:9 that instrumental praise would be in the church. What do we make of the fact that there is no biblical evidence of the fulfillment of that prediction? I do not believe the absence of instruments in the worship of the early church proves that David was a presumptuous prophet. Instead, the absence of instruments indicates that it was never the intention of David to predict that instruments would be used in the church. The absence of instruments from early Christian worship demonstrates that anyone who says the prophets predicted instruments for church worship is declaring a message God did not speak.

Assessment of Atchley's Old Testament Reasons for Using Instrumental Music

So what can be said in summary regarding Atchley's Old Testament reasons for accepting instrumental music in the church?

• First, I agree that according to the Old Testament, God both commanded and accepted instrumental music in worship. However, I object to the insinuation that people who oppose instrumental music for Christian worship do not believe God approved instrumental music under the Old Covenant.

• Second, God's acceptance of instrumental praise under the Old Covenant does not constitute independent authority for its presence in the church's worship. One must find evidence favoring instrumental praise in the New Testament documents that pertain to Christian worship.

• Third, Atchley's efforts to move Old Testament teaching regarding instruments into the New Testament by his appeals to the command to sing psalms, instructions concerning instruments given before the law, and messianic prophecies anticipating instrumental praise are fatally flawed. They constitute no justification for the use of musical instruments in Christian worship.

At this point in his argument, the only truth Atchley has successfully demonstrated is that worship with instruments was commanded and accepted by God under the Old Covenant, a point of view that most a cappella advocates also affirm. However, his arguments to show God's approval of instruments in the worship of the church have failed.

Chapter 2

Evaluating the New Testament Reasons

As he makes the transition from Old Testament reasons for accepting instrumental music to more direct New Testament reasons, Atchley suggests that if God's attitude toward instrumental music reflected in the Old Testament changed in the New Testament one would expect to find one of three things: (1) a clear passage condemning its use; (2) a clear passage commanding a cappella praise only; or (3) a prophecy announcing the end of instrumental music.

The direction of Atchley's argument becomes clear. No New Testament passage explicitly condemns instrumental music. Further, Atchley contends that no New Testament passage commands Christians to "sing only" (a point that will be discussed later). Finally, although he does not pursue the point, there is no prophecy that explicitly announces the end of instrumental music. So, given his criteria and his elaboration of them, God commands and accepts instrumental music for the church today just as he did for Israel under the Old Covenant. However, before one embraces Atchley's criteria and the conclusion they serve for him, some critical matters must be considered.

• First, if these criteria are valid in determining whether or not instrumental music should be practiced in Christian worship, they should be equally valid in determining the propriety of any Old Covenant practice for the church. The shortsightedness of this approach can be recognized when one applies it to other Old Covenant regulations and practices. Consider the commanded execution of a person who curses his father or mother (Leviticus 20:9), the stoning of a blasphemer (24:13-16), and the prohibition of wearing clothing woven of two kinds of material (19:19). All of these were commanded by God in the Old Testament, and, presumably, God was pleased when Israelites obeyed Him in these matters.

The New Testament has no passage that condemns the implementation of any of these directives nor is there a prophecy announcing the end of any of them. Given Atchley's rationale, all could be enjoined on the church. In addition, according to Old Covenant practice, the burning of incense apparently accompanied prayer (Luke 1:10) and was pleasing to God. The New Testament instructs Christians to pray, but it does not command Christians to "pray only." And there is neither an explicit prohibition of incense nor a prophecy predicting its end. Following Atchley's strategy, the assembled church could burn incense to accompany her prayers.

As in the case of other arguments he makes, Atchley thinks this strategy supports the use of instruments in Christian worship, but he seems to be unaware of the baggage this approach carries. Given his strategy, any practice that God enjoined upon and accepted from the Jews under the Old Covenant should be practiced by the church unless countermanded by these criteria. One is left to wonder how brother Atchley would apply his criteria consistently if they constitute the hermeneutical key that determines whether the Old Testament perspective on instrumental praise should be retained or rejected.

• Second, one is at a loss to know the basis for Atchley's criteria. He offers no justification for them; he merely asserts them. It is almost as if he begins with the conclusion he wishes to reach and creates criteria that cannot be met in order to get to his destination. Why could not one say in just as arbitrary a manner and in contrast to Atchley's expectations that if God's attitude toward instrumental music in the Old Testament remained the same in the New Testament, he could expect to find (1) a clear passage advocating its use and/or (2) a clear reference to instrumental music being practiced? One has just as much right to suggest these criteria, and in my mind these are more serviceable.

However, neither of us should arbitrarily declare unjustified criteria on the basis of which such a momentous decision is to be made. The most helpful course is to take the New Testament texts for what they say and determine on the basis of sound methods of interpretation whether they justify instrumental music for Christian worship. With this in mind I turn to a consideration of brother Atchley's New Testament reasons for accepting instrumental praise.

Jesus Does Not Deal With Instrumental Music

Atchley's first New Testament reason for using instrumental music is the fact that Jesus never deals with the issue. While Jesus did address the issue of the sincere heart in worship, Atchley contends, "[H]e never addressed the music issue once."

• In evaluating this component of the argument, I must first question the implicit hermeneutical assumption upon which this point is based, namely, that a subject Jesus does not explicitly address in His teaching is incidental or peripheral. Or to state the assumption in another manner, only those matters that Jesus specifically speaks about are important for Christians.

Are we prepared to accept the implications of this position? There are important matters about which Jesus does not directly speak in the records we have. There are even important issues that Jesus does not speak against. Concerning issues of church practice, where does Jesus ever speak about elders or deacons in churches?[1] Where does Jesus ever speak concerning the continuation or cessation of the Aaronic priesthood? Where does Jesus ever speak concerning sprinkling or pouring as a mode of baptism or the baptism of infants? As far as the biblical evidence goes, Jesus never speaks explicitly to any of these issues.

Concerning ethical issues, where does Jesus ever speak to the issue of a husband's responsibility to love his wife and a wife's responsibility to submit to her husband? Where does He ever speak against homosexual practice? The fact that Jesus does not specifically mention these issues (and any number of others) does not mean they are not important. Why is it different with instrumental praise? The fact that Jesus does not speak about church music does not address the issue of biblical authority for instrumental music in Christian worship. Jesus taught His apostles that some things would be revealed later than His public ministry (John 16:12-14). One should expect important instruction in New Testament literature outside of the Gospels. The New Testament canon is comprised of 27 books, not four.

• Second, it should be pointed out that if non-instrumentalists cannot appeal to the teaching of Jesus in support of their position because Jesus did not deal with the issue, then neither can instrumentalists appeal to Jesus for support of their position. The blade of this knife cuts in both directions.

• This leads me to a third observation concerning one of the most intriguing and puzzling points in Atchley's argument. Despite the fact that he says Jesus "never addressed the music issue once," he surprisingly appeals to Jesus' teaching for support of instrumental praise in the church.

He turns to the parable of the prodigal son in Luke 15:11-32. In particular he calls attention to verse 25 that says the older brother heard music in the celebration at the return of his lost sibling. Atchley points out that the word translated "music" is the Greek word *symphonia* that refers to instrumental music, perhaps music played by a band. He says, "In this powerful metaphor of a prodigal who has come back to the people of God, who is back in the house of God, Jesus says they were having a party and there was a band." Atchley concludes with emphasis, "You would have a hard time, based on what Jesus said, arguing He had a problem with instrumental praise."

Independent of the issue of instrumental music in Christian worship, Atchley's observations regarding the parable in Luke 15 are out of line with the most basic principles of parable interpretation. It is widely recognized among biblical interpreters that all the details of parables must not be pressed for independent spiritual application. Robert Stein writes concerning the parable of the prodigal son as follows:

> [I]n the parable of the prodigal son, such details as the returning son being given a robe, sandals, a signet ring, and a fatted calf for a feast do not possess a corresponding reality. ... These picture parts demonstrate the great love of

the father and his full acceptance of his son. Thus, they help illustrate an aspect of the point of the parable (God's love for the outcasts), but they do not possess any specific meaning in themselves.[2]

Neil Lightfoot adds concerning the interpretation of this parable:

> [I]n the Parable of the Prodigal Son, such things as the fatted calf and the "music and dancing" obviously have no meaning. When studying the ... parable it would be foolish to ask, "What do the swine stand for?" or "What does the ring on the finger represent?" [3]

He then observes, "A failure to recognize that all of the details of a parable are not meaningful has led many astray in their interpretations." [4]

From another angle it should be noticed that Atchley makes much of the older brother's hearing music at the celebration. This convinces him that Jesus certainly approves of instrumental praise in the church. However, he does not mention that the brother heard both music and dancing (Luke 15:25). Luke uses the Greek word *koros*, from which we derive our English word "choreography." The term refers to dancing, perhaps done by a group. Given Atchley's approach, one would have a hard time, based on what Jesus said, arguing he had a problem with dancing as an act of church worship. And should penitent prodigals who return to our congregations be given a ring, a robe, a pair of sandals, and a feast of fattened calf? The truth of the matter is that the mention of music and dancing in the celebration at the return of the prodigal has absolutely nothing to do with praise in the Christian assembly. It simply reflects a typical social celebration in a Jewish family when a wayward son returned home. And it underscores the incomparable joy that God has, and that we should have, when a sinner repents and returns to his Father.[5]

Atchley closes the first stage of his New Testament argument by contending that Jesus taught regularly in the temple and, apparently, did not have a problem with the instruments that were used there. He says, "You will note He did not cast out the musicians with the money changers" – a line that played well with many in his audience but carries no weight at all as an argument for instrumental Christian praise.[6]

These remarks about Jesus' relationship to the temple are equally misdirected. None of the New Testament references to Jesus and the temple indicates He was participating in the temple worship. He may have done that, but it is never explicitly stated in the Gospels that He did. Whether Jesus had a positive or negative attitude toward the temple as an institution continues to be the subject of debate in scholarship.[7] However, He did pay the temple tax (Matthew 17:24-27) and told the cleansed leper to show himself to the priest and to offer the gift Moses commanded (8:4; Luke 5:14). His cleansing of the temple seems to suggest that He desired that the temple serve the purposes God intended for it to serve (Matthew 21:12-13; Mark 11:15-17; Luke 19:45-46; John 2:13-16). Numerous references are made to Jesus' using the temple precincts as a location for teaching. Nevertheless, the Gospels lack explicit evidence that Jesus Himself participated in the temple cult. Even if Jesus participated in worship at the temple, He was an obedient Jew living at a time when temple worship was in force. One would expect Him to have participated in temple activities.[8]

And the fact that Jesus did not cast out the musicians with the money changers is completely irrelevant. Jesus had an issue with the money changers and those who sold sacrifices because they were turning His Father's house into a marketplace (John 2:14-16). Neither did Jesus cast out the priests and the Levites. Surely Atchley does not believe they should be perpetuated in the church because Jesus, apparently, did not have a problem with them. This, too, is "much ado about nothing" in relation to the issue of instrumental Christian worship.

Before I leave this point, it may be worth noting that Jesus did sing with His disciples at the Last Supper. We know that at least one aspect of that meeting became a precedent for the church's eating of the Lord's Supper (1 Corinthians 11:23-26). The occasion closed with Jesus and the disciples singing a hymn (Mark 14:26; Matthew 26:30); however, no evidence suggests that the singing was accompanied by an instrument. Later New Testament references to singing are consistent with this song shared by Jesus and His disciples.

While Jesus did not speak directly about instrumental music in worship, He did speak in principle about religious practices that lack God's authority and rest only on the authority of men. On the basis of Isaiah the prophet, Jesus pointed out that people whose teachings are but the rules taught by men worship in vain (Matthew 15:8-9; Isaiah 29:13). Jesus further noted that His actions and those of John the Baptist were based on the authority of God (from heaven) and not the authority of men (Matthew 21:23-27). The question of whether instrumental music for Christian worship is based on the authority of God or the authority of men is the central issue in this discussion.

Instrumental Music, a Non-Issue in Acts

The second step in Atchley's New Testament argument is that instrumental music is a non-issue in Acts. He says the early disciples met daily in the temple courts and could worship in spirit and truth in the presence of instrumental music.[9] He further suggests that nowhere in Acts is a pattern for musical praise specified.

Here I must emphasize a point made earlier in reference to Jesus' not mentioning instrumental music. Atchley apparently assumes that because Acts does not address the issue of church music it is not important. But Acts does not address a number of issues of great importance in Christian faith and practice, such as the nature of baptism as an act of incorporation into Christ (Romans 6:3-10) and the nature of the Lord's Supper as communion with the body and blood of Jesus (1 Corinthians 10:14-22).[10] Surely we believe these truths inform our understanding and practice of baptism and the Lord's Supper, but neither is addressed in Acts.

The truth is, Acts is not completely silent regarding music in relation to Christian practice. When in jail at Philippi, Paul and Silas were "praying and singing hymns to God" (Acts 16:25). This was not a church assembly. Two Christian men were in a prison. However, the verb *humneo* suggests they were offering verbal musical praise to God. No evidence of instruments is in this passage. Acts does not refer to music in any other setting of the Christian life.

Presumably Atchley's contention is that because the early Christians placed themselves in the temple courts and did not object to instrumental music that was played in temple worship, they found it acceptable for their worship. However, the effort to justify the use of instruments by early Christians on this basis is far from convincing. I call attention again to the caution raised by Jack Lewis that explicit first-century evidence for the use of instruments in temple worship is lacking. Atchley's argument at this point is based on the assumption that instruments were in the temple of the first century, and my evaluation proceeds accordingly.

That disciples in Jerusalem met in the temple courts is uncontested (Acts 2:46; 3:11; 5:12). Although some interpreters believe the earliest Jewish Christians participated in the worship ritual, nothing in these passages describing early Christians' assembling in the temple courts definitively indicates they did. Some interpreters are of the opinion that the earliest Christians, because of their long entrenchment in Judaism, continued to participate in the temple activities for a while. It would take some time for them to grasp fully the theological implications of the death of Christ.[11] But if instrumental music was played in temple worship, it had no bearing on what the early disciples intentionally did in their Christian gatherings in the temple courts or to what was perpetuated in Christian meetings elsewhere. Nothing suggests that the Christians incorporated and perpetuated the instruments in their activities just as there is nothing to suggest they incorporated and perpetuated any number of other elements of Jewish temple liturgy that are not mentioned in Acts. If lack of reference to the early Christians' voicing an objection to instrumental music in temple worship justifies its presence in the church, then lack of reference to their opposition to other temple practices will justify those activities in the church. Surely this argument proves more than Atchley wants to accept.

More difficult to assess than the early Jerusalem Christians' meeting in the temple courts is the apostle Paul's participation in purification rites in the temple (Acts 21:17-26). There is no question that Paul participated in whatever temple ritual was required in the purification of the men who had made a vow. How to explain this act by Paul has long puzzled interpreters.[12] If Atchley's argument that Christians' worshiping in the temple courts justifies instrumental music for the church, then certainly Paul's participation in the purification rites constitutes a precedent for the church to practice such rites today. However, absolutely no biblical evidence shows that such a practice was implemented or should be implemented in the life of the church.

Whatever the extent of early Christians' involvement with the temple, it ended in A.D. 70 when the Romans destroyed the temple. There is no indication that the activities of the temple cult were continued in the church. In fact, the evidence suggests that they were not.

Instrumental Music, Neither Prescribed nor Prohibited

Third, Atchley argues that the New Testament commands to sing neither prescribe nor prohibit instrumental music. As he transitions from his second point, Atchley says that nowhere in the New Testament is congregational singing specifically authorized. He bases his argument on his interpretation of three passages.

> Do not get drunk on wine, which leads to debauchery. Instead be filled with the Spirit. Speak to one another with psalms, hymns and spiritual songs. Sing and make music in your heart to the Lord (Ephesians 5:18-19).

> Let the word of Christ dwell in you richly as you teach and admonish one another with all wisdom, and as you sing psalms, hymns and spiritual songs with gratitude in your hearts to God (Colossians 3:16).

> Is any one of you in trouble? He should pray. Is anyone happy? Let him sing songs of praise (James 5:13).

Atchley contends that all of these references are speaking to the individual concerning his daily walk and relation to other believers. None of these passages has to do with a Christian assembly in his view.[13]

That the James passage refers to an individual's personal expression of joy is clear from the question "Is anyone happy?" and the following admonition, "Let him sing songs of praise." Although the verse does not preclude a person's expressing his joy with other people, it does not require it. However, the case is different with the passages in Ephesians and Colossians. Unlike the passage in James that may refer to either a private or a collective expression of joy in song, the passages in Ephesians and Colossians point to a person's singing with others.

It is true that both of these texts occur in passages that are devoted to ethical conduct. Ephesians 4-6 delineates ways Christians are to "live a life worthy of the calling [we] have received" (Ephesians 4:1). And Colossians 3:1-4:6 spells out how people who have been "raised with Christ" (3:1) should live. Obviously, the passages have to do with individual Christian responsibility. However, some individual conduct is, by its nature, played out in a relational setting with other people. For example, Paul's instructions to wives and husbands must be obeyed by individual Christian wives and husbands (Ephesians 5:22-33; Colossians 3:18-19). However, the commands and compliance with them assume that husbands and wives are with one another in a relationship. The commands cannot be carried out independent of the relationship of two individuals in marriage.

Similarly the instructions regarding singing imply a communal setting in order to be carried out. Ephesians 5:19 says Christians are to "speak to one another" in various types of songs. Colossians 3:16 indicates that various types of songs are to be sung in a setting that involves "teach(ing) and admonish(ing) one another." The word translated "one another" in both of these passages is the reflexive pronoun *heautou*, used in the sense of the reciprocal pronoun *allelon*.[14] Paul's idea is not of a person singing to himself or within himself but of people singing to each other. Ferguson has written correctly concerning these passages:

> In any case it is not a private religious exercise which is described. The statements accord well with the description of a worship assembly in 1 Corinthians 14 where the activity of the Spirit results in various types of speaking, song, and prayer, and where the emphasis is on understandable verbal edification (done for one another). The assembly of the church is part of the Christian life, and indeed Paul sees it as important in counteracting the problems confronting these churches in Asia to whom the letters are sent. Thus he quite naturally includes references to what was done in the public worship in discussing the expression of the corporate life of Christians in their relations one with another.[15]

To deny the communal nature of the language of Ephesians 5:18-19 and Colossians 3:16, as brother Atchley does, is to deny the obvious. In comments on Colossians 3:16, F.F. Bruce repeatedly draws attention to the context of the language in the lives of the Colossian Christians. Paul is writing about activities that took place "in their meetings," "when they came together," "in their church meetings," "when early Christians came together for worship." [16] And Ferguson has pointed out that in Ephesians 5 and Colossians 3, "although the literary setting is the Christian life, something from the assembly (singing) is used to reinforce the point." [17]

• *A Red Herring.* Atchley next brings 1 Corinthians 14:26 into his argument: "When you come together, everyone has a hymn." He says this passage is the only New Testament reference to music in the assembly, and instead of referring to congregational singing it refers to the singing of a solo. It is difficult to understand how this is an argument for instrumental music. However, it appears that Atchley thinks this text is a problem for a cappella advocates. He says, "Isn't it ironic? The only music mentioned specifically in the assembly in the New Testament is solos, which I guarantee you are forbidden in churches that have the anti-instrument position!"

Atchley's explanation that the expression "everyone has a hymn" (1 Corinthians 14:26) refers to someone's singing a solo is not definitive. He says this means that God had given someone a song to sing, and the person then would sing that song in the assembly. Although Atchley's explanation is a possibility, it certainly is not the only way the passage can be viewed.[18] The language could suggest that a person had a psalm[19] (whether selected from the Old Testament psalter, composed by himself or another Christian, or revealed to him by the Spirit) that he would present for the congregation to sing. Or it could refer to a person's singing parts of the psalm and the congregation's offering a response by singing other parts of the psalm. The fact of the matter is there is not enough evidence for us to know exactly how this was done at Corinth. But however it was done, whether by a solo, by a person's selecting a psalm for the congregation to sing or teaching them a psalm to sing, or participating in a responsorial singing of a psalm, the passage suggests that only singing was done. The action that is described is the intelligible communication of ideas by means of song. There is no evidence of the use of instruments in this passage. Lewis pointed out, "if only 1 Corinthians 14 could be cited as authorization for singing and should singing be reduced to solos, the New Testament still would have nothing to say about using instrumental music."[20]

By his line of argument based on 1 Corinthians 14:26, Atchley places himself and the RH church in somewhat of a bind. If congregational singing is not authorized in the New Testament, as Atchley contends, then on whose authority does the RH church sing congregationally? Further, Atchley says the only passage that authorizes singing in the assembly is 1 Corinthians 14:26 and it authorizes only a solo. Is solo the only kind of singing practiced at RH? Given Atchley's argument, RH's practice of congregational singing is not based on the authority of the New Testament.[21]

I do not believe brother Atchley thinks the RH church does something that God does not approve when they sing congregationally. The problem is he does not explain how congregational singing can be approved by God without God's having in some way instructed Christians to practice it. Remember, Atchley has said that the most important question to consider is "Is a practice biblical?" However, he has failed to explain how congregational singing can be biblical without God's authorizing it. In my mind all this discussion concerning congregational singing not being authorized is a "red herring" that diverts one's mind from the issue at hand, namely, the biblical authority for instrumental music as Christian praise. Atchley's task is not to justify congregational singing or solos in church. The task he has accepted is to show that instrumental music is justified for Christian worship. This he has so far failed to do.

• *It's All About the Context.* Atchley further contends that New Testament commands to sing do not mean to "sing only a cappella." To say that sing means "to sing only" is a human inference, according to Atchley. He seeks to bolster this point by raising the question, "Would early Christians, especially in view of their knowledge of the Old Testament, have concluded that sing meant to sing only unaccompanied?" He then exclaims that we do not use the word sing that way today. Suppose, he says, we invite people to come out to a ranch for a picnic where we are going to sing some songs. Such an invitation would not mean that we would expect to sing only. Someone may bring his guitar along. Playing instruments along with the singing would not be excluded. Therefore, through the back door of our alleged contemporary use of the word "sing"

Atchley draws conclusions regarding the New Testament connotation of the word "sing." His remarks invite three observations.

• First, as has been documented earlier in this book, the earliest Christians did not use instruments in their assemblies, their knowledge of the Old Testament notwithstanding. If their understanding was as Atchley suggests, how does one explain convincingly the absence of instruments from their worship for hundreds of years? Apparently they understood the language when used in reference to their worship to involve vocal music but not instrumental music.

• Second, as demonstrated earlier in the discussion of the Hebrew word *zamar*, sometimes the language of the Old Testament means simply to sing without any necessity of the involvement of instruments. The same can be shown by an investigation of the Greek word *psallo* that appears in the Greek translation of the Old Testament. Early Christians knowledgeable of the Old Testament would have understood the various uses of the terms. In fact, there is evidence that shows that before and during the New Testament period the language was used in some contexts of Jewish praise to mean simply to sing.[22]

• Third, Atchley's argument from the way we use the English word "sing" is unconvincing. Foremost it is irrelevant because we are ultimately concerned about how words were used in the biblical languages, not in English. However, his remarks on the English word "sing," though eloquent, are inaccurate and thereby misleading to those who are hearing his argument. Brother Atchley fails to recognize that words have meaning based on the contexts in which they are used. What is associated with the word "sing" depends on the setting envisioned.

Take as an example what occurred when I attended a church-related camp as a teenager. In the early evening we would go to "the point" where we had a daily devotional. Among other activities in those devotionals we would sing. Because the camp was operated by individuals from churches of Christ, the worship practices were basically consistent with what typically occurred in the churches of Christ from which the campers had come. When it was said that we would sing at the devotional, everyone understood that we would only sing and not play instruments, for that is what the word "sing" connoted in that socio-religious setting.

Later in the evening we would go to other locations around the camp and engage in other activities, sometimes singing. When it was said we were going to the gully or to the mess hall for games and singing, it was understood that singing might involve playing instruments in accompaniment because that was what we typically did in those gatherings that were not dedicated to Christian worship but to social fellowship and entertainment.

And further, one of our male counselors had a Dodge automobile with a powerful motor. When he would rev up the engine and take off down the road, we might say, "Clyde had that Dodge 'singing.' " In this case the word sing did not even refer to someone verbalizing a song, whether accompanied or unaccompanied by an instrument. This was a metaphorical use of the word.

As this description of activities demonstrates, our use of the English word "sing" sometimes conveys the idea of singing only while at other times it refers to accompanied song.[23] And sometimes the word has a metaphorical use that has nothing to do with the human voice or a musical instrument. However, our current use of the English word "sing" is ultimately irrelevant to this issue. What is relevant is the significance of the Greek language as it is used in the pertinent New Testament passages. In the contexts of Jewish and Christian worship of the New Testament period and specifically in the contexts of the passages brother Atchley has cited, it is widely agreed by those who have no axe to grind that the language used to designate musical practice refers to vocal music, not instrumental. Commenting on the occurrence of *psallo* in Ephesians 5:19, Andrew Lincoln writes, "although its original meaning involved plucking a stringed instrument, [*psallo*] here means to make music by singing (cf. also 1 Cor. 14:15; Jas. 5:13), so that there is no reference in this verse to instrumental accompaniment."[24]

Instrumental Music in Heaven

Atchley next contends that instrumental music in the church's worship is biblical because the New Testament refers to instrumental music in heaven.[25] He cites in support of his point the following passages:

> And when he [the Lamb] had taken it [the scroll], the four living creatures and the twenty-four elders fell down before

the Lamb. Each one had a harp and they were holding bowls full of incense, which are the prayers of the saints (Revelation 5:8).

And I saw what looked like a sea of glass mixed with fire and, standing beside the sea, those who had been victorious over the beast and his image and over the number of his name. They held harps given them by God and sang the song of Moses the servant of God and the song of the Lamb (Revelation 15:2-3).

Atchley says that it is immaterial whether the instruments mentioned in these passages are literal or figurative. He asks, "Am I honestly to believe that what God is enjoying right now in heaven He is despising on earth?" Because God enjoys instrumental music in heaven, Atchley contends He approves of it in the church on earth.

My evaluation of this line of argument focuses on two important matters that underscore the fact that it is not the intention of the visions of Revelation to delineate congregational worship practices in general or instrumental praise in particular.

• First, if we are serious about reading Scripture responsibly, we must take into consideration the genre, or literary type, of the document we are reading. The Bible is composed of narratives, law codes, poems, epistles, parables, prophecy, wisdom sayings and apocalypses. Each has its own rules of interpretation and to fail to recognize these rules is to invite confusion. Robert Stein has observed, "If we are not aware of the rules under which the biblical author wrote, misinterpretation almost certainly will take place." [26]

In the case of an apocalypse like Revelation, instead of whether the instruments are literal or figurative being immaterial, as Atchley suggests, this is, in fact, a fundamental point that must be considered in the interpretation of these passages. We must not dismiss the symbolic nature of language in Revelation. Klein, Blomberg and Hubbard, three respected evangelical writers on biblical interpretation, have warned as follows:

> Most importantly we must recognize that Revelation employs highly symbolic and figurative imagery that we dare

not interpret too literally. Virtually every reader recognizes this in the most obvious instances .... But it is amazing how often these same readers do not recognize that they should interpret the other images in the book as equally symbolic.[27]

We can recognize the symbolic nature of language in Revelation by a careful consideration of the literary context in which it occurs. In the case of Revelation 5:8 the symbolic imagery is apparent. Here we encounter the Lamb that looked as if it had been slain and that had seven horns and seven eyes, which are the seven spirits of God (5:6). Further, there are the 24 elders holding golden bowls of incense, which, the text says, "are the prayers of the saints" (5:8). It would seem on any reading of Revelation 5 that the Lamb is symbolic of Jesus, the seven eyes are metaphorical for the spirit of God or the presence of God, and the bowls of incense are a metaphor for the prayers of the saints. It is reasonable to understand that the harps the elders hold (5:8) are no less metaphorical, symbols of praise.

Similar observations can be made regarding Revelation 15. In introducing the vision John says, "I saw in heaven another great and marvelous sign" (v. 1). The term "sign" suggests that the vision he saw signified, pointed to, or symbolized some entity. He saw something that "looked like" a sea of glass mixed with fire (v. 2). And there are the harps held by those who sang the song of Moses and the song of the Lamb (vv. 2-4). Note the simile in Revelation 14:2 for further support of the likely figurative understanding of the harps. The sound that John heard was "like that of harpists playing their harps." Concerning the references to harps in Revelation, William Sheppard Smith has correctly noted, "Like the incense, however, the harps are only symbolic, reflecting the Jewish temple worship."[28]

• My second observation is this, if it is granted that whether the harps are literal or figurative is immaterial, it is not for the reason Atchley suggests. The point is immaterial because there is no convincing reason why one should assume that Revelation's visions of heaven describe what should literally take place in the assembly of the church. As Delling has pointed out, "The ref(erences) to stringed instruments in heavenly worship at Rev. 5:8; 15:2 ... need not mean that such instruments might sometimes accompany the singing at primitive Chr(istian) Worship." [29]

If the references to harps in Revelation 5:8 and 15:2-3 mean that there should be instruments in the church, why do not the references to other things also justify their presence in the church? Why should a church not have 24 elders (no more or no less) who, instead of sitting inconspicuously among the congregation, wear white garments and gold crowns and sit on thrones (4:4)? Why should the church in her worship not actually burn incense in bowls (5:8)? And why does the church not model her affairs after the tabernacle and the temple that have a visible presence in the vision of Revelation 15:5-8? As Price has insightfully pointed out, "The same argument that would bring the harps into the church must also bring all these other aspects of worship as well. The apostle John is speaking figuratively of heaven's worship under the image of the Old Testament Temple." [30]

Atchley, like other instrumental music advocates who have made this argument, has failed to present a methodology that successfully explains how one part of these visionary descriptions of heaven in Revelation, namely the harps, justifies a church practice, while all the other parts of the descriptions do not. Brian Schwertley, a Presbyterian, has appropriately noted, "Therefore, the book of Revelation no more authorizes the use of musical instruments in public worship than it does incense, altars, trumpets, or sacrificial temples. One cannot arbitrarily accept one without accepting the others also." [31]

The New Testament Idea of Giftedness

Atchley's fifth line of argument concerns the New Testament idea of giftedness. He offers no biblical theology of giftedness to provide a context for his discussion. He merely questions, "If God was honored by the contributions of gifted musicians in the Old Testament, why not now?" He asks further, "Why make it difficult for our own members who just want to serve God?"

In response it should again be noted that God's acceptance of worship from gifted instrumental musicians under the Old Covenant does not prove that instrumental music is authorized for Christian worship. One must show the evidence for instrumental music in the documents that speak to the use of music in Christian worship.[32]

Further, we must recognize that all a Christian does is to be done in honor of God. "Whatever you do, work at it with all your heart, as working for the Lord, not for men" (Colossians 3:23). Many Christians have exceptional abilities in any number of areas, and these abilities should be exercised in honor of God (1 Peter 4:10-11). However, not all of our abilities and gifts are to be exercised as acts of worship in the assembled church.[33]

Let me note something related to the music issue. Atchley has said much about the playing of instruments in the Old Testament by gifted musicians having been accepted by God, and he has pleaded for the church to allow such playing by gifted musicians to take place in the church's worship. One should recognize that along with the several instruments identified in the Old Testament as vehicles of praise to God, dancing is also listed as an act of praise or an act accompanying praise. Psalm 150, which Atchley quoted earlier to demonstrate the Old Testament's approval of instrumental praise, is a case in point. The psalmist declares:

> Praise him with the sounding of the trumpet, praise him with the harp and lyre, praise him with tambourine and dancing, praise him with the strings and flute, praise him with the clash of cymbals, praise him with resounding cymbals (Psalm 150:3-5).

Also note Psalm 149:3 which says, "Let them praise his name with dancing and make music to him with tambourine and harp." And in the case of Exodus 15:20, a passage that mentions instruments before the law was given, Miriam and the women not only played their tambourines but also danced.

I am not gifted in respect to dancing, but some people are. Why should the church not allow such gifted dancers to exercise their talent in the service of God, especially because in the Old Testament God commanded and accepted praise from sincere and gifted dancers?

A significant movement is occurring in some religious circles in the area of liturgical dance. Websites offer instruction concerning choreography and costuming for religious dance. Many of them also offer their biblical justification for dance as a part of church liturgy. The arguments they present sound amazingly familiar.

Churches of Christ in general and the RH church in particular historically have not practiced sacred dance in our assemblies. However, given the line of reasoning that brother Atchley has followed in support of instrumental music and the line of argument that the RH elders have endorsed unanimously, dancing should be equally acceptable as an act of church worship. Consider these justifications for dancing in church:

- Dancing was commanded and accepted by God in the Old Testament (Psalm 149:3; 150:3-5) and is never explicitly forbidden in the New Testament. Neither is there a prophecy that predicted the end of dance as an expression of praise.
- Dancing was offered to and accepted by God in the Old Testament before the giving of the law (Exodus 15:20); therefore, the practice should transcend to the new covenant.
- Dancing is mentioned in Psalms (149:3; 150:4), the very psalms we are commanded to read and sing in the New Testament.
- Dancing is mentioned in the context of Old Testament passages that are quoted messianically in the New Testament (Jeremiah 31:15; Matthew 2:17-18; Jeremiah 31:31-34; Hebrews 8:8-12; 10:16-17). See the reference to tambourines and dance in Jeremiah 31:4, 13.
- Jesus did not speak against dancing. He actually approved of dancing by mentioning it in the parable of the prodigal son (Luke 15:25). Further, if temple practice in Jesus' day followed Old Testament precedents, dancing would have taken place. Because Jesus did not drive out the dancers, He must approve dancing for the church.
- Dancing is a non-issue in Acts. Because early Christians attended the temple, they must not have had a problem with dancing in worship that took place there.
- Dancing accompanied singing in Old Testament worship. And in today's culture, singing and dancing often go hand-in-glove. Because the New Testament does not command us to "sing only," then dancing should be allowed to accompany the singing in the church.
- Some Christians are gifted as dancers and should be allowed to use their gift in serving God.
- Because dancing is widely accepted in our culture, it could be a way of reaching more people.

Practically every argument Atchley makes in support of RH's adding an instrumental music service could be made in support of adding a dancing service. And he has offered no hermeneutical insight that reveals why they should not.

Suppose some RH members who considered themselves gifted as dancers expressed their desire to use that gift in their worship of God. They would not be able to do that in the assemblies at RH under the present arrangement, as I understand it. These talented and gifted Christians would have to leave, perhaps finding an opportunity at a church that has a liturgical dance group. Would RH provide an opportunity in one of their assemblies for these persons to serve God with their gift of dance as a means of keeping them from leaving? I suspect that what I have described is purely hypothetical and no one has left RH because he/she wanted to dance in church. But why should people so gifted not be able to dance in church? Again, Atchley has offered no hermeneutical guide that will allow one who holds his position to resolve this problem? [34]

Of course the issue of one's giftedness is beside the point in the case for or against instrumental music in Christian worship. This argument is essentially an emotional appeal that takes a person's mind away from the more fundamental issue of whether a particular activity can be included in Christian worship on the basis of sound biblical argument. If it can be, then one's giftedness in that area of action can legitimately be employed in the church's worship. If, on the other hand, the activity lacks biblical sanction for inclusion in Christian worship, then one's giftedness in that regard should not be used in the assembly of the church. This is not a disenfranchisement of the gifted person. It is simply recognition of God's authority.

Assessment of Atchley's New Testament Reasons for Instrumental Music

None of Atchley's New Testament reasons for accepting instrumental music constitutes a biblical justification for its inclusion in Christian worship. One finds these arguments compromised by imprecision, inaccuracy and inconsistency similar to what is found in his Old Testament reasons.

Chapter 3

Plumbing the Bottom Line

As brother Atchley comes to the end of his biblical case for instrumental music, he refers to what he calls "the bottom line" of the issue. He says, "The authority to forbid instrumental music must be established apart from a clear command of God. You can't open your Bible and show me where God forbids it." Further he says, "All the e-mails I got from critics never mentioned the verse where God forbids or condemns instrumental praise, because it's not there." [1]

With these remarks Atchley has shifted the focus of the argument. The task that he has taken up is that of demonstrating that the Scriptures justify the use of instruments of music in the church's worship. Over the years non-instrumental brethren have pleaded with instrumental music advocates to show the verse where God commands or approves instrumental music for Christian worship. They have yet to cite it. None of the arguments that brother Atchley has made identifies the verse that unquestionably demonstrates that instrumental music is approved for worship in the church. Like instrumental music advocates before him, he has shifted the focus from his responsibility to provide authority for the instrument to the responsibility of the non-instrumentalists to provide "the authority to forbid instrumental music."

I do not believe Atchley realizes what he is conceding by resorting to this strategy. By resting his case here he is implying that all the arguments he has made up to this point have not been successful. Remember, brother Atchley says that the most important question is, "Is instrumental praise biblical?" He then presents "reasons," both from the Old Testament and from the New, for accepting instrumental music. One is led to believe that he thinks his arguments demonstrate that God approves instrumental praise for the church's assembly.

But this constitutes a problem for Atchley's case. If it can be shown that there is clear positive authorization for instrumental music in Christian worship (as Atchley believes he has done), then there is no need to appeal to the absence of a prohibition against it (as he does). It is nonsensical to think that God would clearly instruct Christians to use instruments then explicitly prohibit them from doing so. This is another indication of internal inconsistency that haunts Atchley's case. But there are other problems with this argument.

In support of his view Atchley makes his assessment of Everett Ferguson's work that I alluded to earlier. I quote his remarks in full because it is crucial for one to recognize how Atchley uses Ferguson's language. He says:

> Probably the best-written book to defend a cappella music in the last century was by Everett Ferguson, a beautiful man that teaches at ACU. In his book, *A Cappella Music in the Public Worship of the Church*, he honestly admits on page 40 and 41, "Before leaving the New Testament references, we may note in passing that the New Testament gives no negative judgment on instrumental music per se. ... The situation is simply that instruments are not referred to in the church's worship." I would say, yes. It was a non-issue. They're not spoken about positively; they're not spoken about negatively. They're not prescribed; they're not precluded. It wasn't even an issue. It never dawned on them that it was an issue.

Atchley has pleaded for people to let the biblical writers say what they say and not make them say more than they say. I would agree; that is good counsel. However, that counsel should also guide us in reading and using the writings of non-biblical authors. It is a flawed biblical hermeneutic that fails to take into consideration the context of a biblical passage. It is an equally flawed argument to use a statement from a non-biblical author without adequately recognizing the context in which the statement is made. Such selective quoting can be self-serving for an advocate and misleading to those who are listening to him.

Atchley's elaboration on Ferguson's remarks gives the impression that Ferguson's acknowledgement that there is no prohibition against instrumental music per se in the New Testament naturally leads to the conclusion that Atchley reaches regarding the issue of instrumental praise. Atchley quotes Ferguson and says, in essence, "See there; that's my point; the issue of instrumental music in worship did not matter to them!" I do not believe this is an appropriate use of Ferguson's work.

Atchley quotes only two sentences from a book of approximately 100 pages in which Ferguson argues a case *for* non-instrumental Christian worship, *not for* instrumental Christian worship. And as my transcription of Atchley's remarks shows by the ellipsis, he omits part of Ferguson's statement that, if present, would allow the reader to understand better the point he is actually making. Ferguson's entire statement is as follows, with the lines omitted by Atchley in italics:

> Before leaving the New Testament references, we may note in passing that the New Testament gives no negative judgment on instrumental music per se. *It makes neutral references to playing on instruments (Matthew 11:17 and parallels), uses instruments as illustrations (1 Corinthians 13:1; 14:7f., with unfavorable connotations it may be noted), and compares the heavenly worship to the sound of instruments (Revelation 14:2f, probably under the influence of Old Testament and Temple practice). A parallel to the last reference may be seen in Revelation 5:8 with its figurative use of incense from the temple worship.* The situation is simply that instruments are not referred to in the church's worship.[2]

The assessment of evidence that Atchley quotes reflects one of the hallmarks of Ferguson's scholarship, namely, his effort to be open and fair with evidence. What Ferguson says should be recognized by anyone who reads the New Testament. There is no explicit prohibition of instrumental music per se. But remember, instrumental music per se is not the issue of this discussion.[3] Ferguson is simply pointing out that although instrumental music is mentioned in a number of settings in the New Testament, it is not mentioned in the context of Christian worship, which is the point at issue in this inquiry.

The weight of Ferguson's work is the relevant linguistic, historical and theological evidence that he presents. I will quote other statements from Ferguson's work that will place the lines Atchley quotes in a broader context. Ferguson writes:

> According to the New Testament evidence instrumental music was not present in the worship of the early church. Singing incontestably was present in the corporate life of the early Christians (1 Corinthians 14:15, 26; Colossians 3:15 ff.; Ephesians 5:18 ff.) and this was rooted in the practice of Jesus with his disciples (Mark 14:26). But there is no clear reference to instrumental music in Christian worship in any New Testament text.[4]

> Personally, I am convinced that later ecclesiastical usage and Jewish usage before and contemporary with the New Testament confirm a reference to vocal music exclusively in the New Testament texts. This is substantiated by the failure of the great majority of translators, lexicographers, commentators, and historians of church music to find a clear reference to instrumental music in the church's worship in any New Testament text.[5]

> So, no instrument is found in the New Testament reference, but only vocal praise, and thus no New Testament authority for instrumental music in worship is available.[6]

> The conclusion drawn from the New Testament texts and from linguistic evidence was that instrumental music was not present in the worship of the New Testament church. This conclusion has further support in the contextual setting of

New Testament times. Jewish practices and attitudes (both Rabbinic and Hellenistic) furnish strong presumption against the presence of instrumental music in the early church.[7]

As Ferguson begins to evaluate the evidence of early post-New Testament Christian history, he notes that there is "a consistent reference to singing but an absence of any reference to playing."[8] As he continues his survey he writes:

> The conclusion that the early church did not employ instrumental music in worship does not rest, however, on inferences from silence. There are explicit statements from early Christian writers to the effect that Christians did not use instrumental music. Lest anyone be misled by citations which might imply a use of instrumental music in the church, I cite here some of the explicit evidence against such use. Although it would be bold to say that an instrument was never used by Christians in their public assemblies, I can say that if it was, it was exceptional and unusual.[9]

At the end of his chapter on the evidence from early church history Ferguson writes:

> Historical evidence makes it most unlikely that an instrument can be found in *psallo* in the New Testament and shows that the absence of any reference to instrumental music in the church's worship in early days was not accidental. It was not mentioned because it was not there. There is no time when one can point to an original use of instruments in the church being abandoned.[10]

I have quoted from Ferguson at length in order to emphasize that the absence from the New Testament of a prohibition against instrumental music per se does not necessitate the conclusion that brother Atchley has reached, namely, that instrumental praise was an issue of no consequence to the New Testament writers. Further, the absence of references to instruments as vehicles of praise should not be construed as permission to employ them in Christian worship without persuasive evidence that they should be so used.

To see the contrast between Atchley's position and that of Ferguson, note again Ferguson's remark in the last quotation, "the absence of any reference to instrumental music in the church's worship in the early days was not accidental." Atchley's view is that the biblical writers were not really concerned about the nature of the music offered in Christian worship. He provides no evidence for his conclusion; he simply affirms it. Ferguson, on the other hand, presents a well-documented and well-argued case that supports his contention that the silence of the New Testament concerning instruments in worship is not merely incidental. Summarizing his case he writes:

> Have we read the New Testament correctly? This can be checked in part by the interpretation of the New Testament in early Christian writings and by the practice of the post-New Testament church. Is it an accident that we have no clear reference to instrumental music in the church's worship in the New Testament? Was instrumental music actually used but not referred to? The answer of history is "no." What is an inference from the New Testament evidence, and the presumption from the church's setting in the context of Judaism, is made explicit in the testimony from church history. When our conclusions about the New Testament evidence concerning the use of the instrument are checked by the writings of the early church, we once more find a negative result.[11]

Atchley essentially rests his case for instruments in Christian worship on the absence of an explicit New Testament prohibition against their use. His "bottom line" argument is not to present the positive evidence for the use of instruments, for there is none. If there were such evidence, Atchley would not need to appeal to the absence of a prohibition against instruments. At the end of the day he bases his initiative to add instruments to Christian worship on the fact that there is no prohibition against their use in the New Testament. We can use instruments, he suggests, because the New Testament never says we cannot.

As I evaluate this argument further, I am wondering why Atchley and the RH elders do not follow it with respect to other issues. I have a publication from the RH church titled "Does Anything Happen at Baptism?" [12] Atchley may have written the article, although it does not carry his name. I assume he agrees with the article's content. The article claims that the RH church believes that infants should not be baptized, either as a means of forgiving sins or as a dedicatory rite.[13]

I am struck by the fact that nowhere in the New Testament can one find a statement that explicitly condemns or forbids infant baptism. One finds positive teaching that sanctions the baptism of penitent believers, which the RH article appropriately cites, but there is not one word of explicit condemnation of infant baptism in the New Testament. Should the RH church now approve infant baptism because there is no passage in the New Testament that says, "We can't do it?" Should they become a both/and church and offer both believer's baptism and infant baptism? I think they would be the first to say they should not. Why then have they accepted instrumental music simply because the New Testament never condemns it? The only instruction in the New Testament concerning the age of a person who should be baptized is the positive directive to baptize people who are old enough to have heard the gospel, believed it and repented. That is sufficient, without any evidence to the contrary, to exclude infants. And the only instruction in the New Testament concerning music in Christian worship is the positive authorization to sing and make melody in the heart. Without any positive evidence to the contrary, that should be sufficient to exclude the use of instruments as vehicles of praise.

If one embraces Atchley's "bottom line" argument for instrumental music in Christian worship, he must be prepared to accept its implications. The "you can't show me where it says I can't" argument is, indeed, liberating. Show me where the New Testament forbids or condemns sprinkling as a mode of baptism. Where does it forbid infant baptism, a pope as the head of the church on earth, a regional bishop over several congregations, or burning incense as an act of Christian worship? Against none of these can a person find an explicit prohibition in the New Testament. I have no reason to think Atchley and the RH elders are advocates for any of these practices. However, the "you can't show me where the Bible says I can't" argument for the instrument will also justify these practices for the church. Unless Atchley can show why instruments should be accepted and these other practices should not be accepted, his case fails.

John Price has assessed the case accurately as follows:

> The Bible affirms that worship is always a matter of what God commands, never a matter of what He has forbidden. It is not enough to show that musical instruments are not forbidden; it must be shown that God has positively commanded them. ...
>
> ... In the same way that He has not forbidden the use of musical instruments in the New Testament, He has not forbidden the eating of meat at His Supper. All would agree that to eat meat at the Lord's Supper would be a presumptuous addition to His will. But if we use the rule that what is not forbidden is acceptable, then to eat meat at the Lord's Supper must be admissible. Why should the addition of musical instruments in His worship be viewed any differently than the addition of eating meat at His Supper? The argument that because musical instruments are not forbidden in the New Testament and, therefore, acceptable must be dismissed.[14]

Chapter 4

Psallo and Silence

Brother Atchley closes his lesson with responses to what he regards as the two major arguments for the anti-instrument position – (1) the *psallo* argument; (2) the argument from silence or the law of exclusion.[1]

The *Psallo* Argument

Psallo is a Greek verb that appears five times in four New Testament passages (Romans 15:9; 1 Corinthians 14:15 [twice]; Ephesians 5:19; James 5:13). The word found a place in the church music issue in the late 19th century when some individuals began to contend that the verb means to play an instrument or to sing accompanied by an instrument. They appealed to this meaning as justification for the use of instruments in church worship.

Other individuals assessed the evidence concerning *psallo* and concluded that the term, as it is used in the New Testament, does not imply the use of mechanical instruments. The *"psallo* argument" made by brothers who opposed mechanical instruments was essentially a response to the *"psallo* argument" initially made by the instrumentalists.

Brother Atchley places himself in the tradition of those who understand *psallo* to embrace the use of a mechanical instrument as per its New Testament usage, as his further discussion at this point in his argument shows. He takes issue with the perspectives on *psallo* that have been offered from the a cappella camp. He explains the argument propounded by a cappella advocates as follows:

> The term originally meant "to pluck, then to play a stringed instrument," and this meaning is reflected in the Greek Old Testament. But, the anti-instrumental people say that on the street by the first century, *psallo* had evolved to include the idea of making music with the voice. And some contend that it only meant that by the first century, and that this is how Paul intended it to be understood.

Assessing this argument Atchley says, "Now you can read articles about this until you are tired in the head, but I will just tell you the bulk of scholarship disagrees." He offers no references from the "bulk of scholarship" he has in mind, so people who are hearing his argument have nothing to go on except his affirmation. He says further that in the works of the ancient writers Josephus, Suetonius, Chrysostom, Gregory of Nyssa and in the Septuagint the term *psallo* is clearly used to mean "to play an instrument." He does not offer any specific citation from any of these sources, so again he provides no basis for evaluation.[2]

Atchley and other recent instrumental music advocates appear to be following the lead of Tom Burgess who in his *Documents on Instrumental Music* intentionally reacts to comments regarding the verb *psallo* made by M.C. Kurfees, a non-instrumentalist who wrote in the early 20th century.[3] Kurfees contended:

> [T]he Greek word *psallo* once meant to pluck the hair, twang the bowstring, twitch a carpenter's line, and to touch the chords of a musical instrument, but had entirely lost all of these meanings before the beginning of the New Testament period, and that, therefore, the word is never used in the New Testament nor in contemporaneous literature in any of these senses. At this time, it not only meant to sing, but that is the only sense in which it was used, all the other meanings have entirely disappeared.[4]

Kurfees' work was significant in that it called attention to the fact that words have a history in a living language and a word's meaning may change with the passing of time and through various uses. He demonstrated that this was the case with *psallo*. Kurfees showed that the term which early meant to pluck or twitch various objects came to be used of plucking the strings of a musical instrument, then of singing a song with the accompaniment of an instrument, then simply of singing a song. This reality is solidly recognized in current scholarship, as my later discussion will show. However, Kurfees made himself vulnerable to criticism by leaving the impression that the word *psallo* was never used in an instrumental context in non-biblical Greek writings of the New Testament period and subsequently. In light of the evidence, Kurfees seems to have overstated his case. His overstatement has been recognized by a cappella advocates for a long time.

Atchley thinks Everett Ferguson has written the best defense of the a cappella position and should be aware of the fact that Ferguson offers a more balanced assessment of the linguistic evidence than Kurfees provided. Ferguson cites sources written in Greek contemporaneous with the late New Testament period and following that use *psallo* in its classical sense of playing an instrument. However, Ferguson also cites evidence that demonstrates that in some Jewish religious contexts *psallo* had increasingly taken on the meaning of vocal expression. He summarizes the evidence by saying, "The classical meaning of *psallo* continued into Hellenistic and post-New Testament times. ... Conversely, *psallo* with the simple meaning 'sing' or 'sing praise' ('sing the psalms') is well attested before the New Testament times."[5] He then demonstrates that the uses of *psallo* in the New Testament reflect the Jewish religious use rather than the classical use of the word.[6] He further demonstrates that this vocal understanding is confirmed by post-apostolic Christian writings.[7]

Earlier Wm. M. Green had recognized the extreme nature of Kurfees' statement. He observed, "It is possible ... to admit that Kurfees claimed too much, without admitting ... that *psallo* in the New Testament necessarily means to sing with the instrument."[8]

Atchley dismisses the evidence for a vocal understanding of *psallo* with a wave of the hand against the unfortunately extreme statement by Kurfees and says, "the bulk of scholarship disagrees." He fails, however, to present to his hearers what scholarship does, in fact, say about the various uses of the verb *psallo* in general and its particular use in the contexts of Jewish worship and Christian worship in the New Testament period.

Atchley's observations regarding *psallo* suffer from the same imprecise methodology that plague his discussion of the Hebrew word *zamar*.[9] As in that case, Atchley appears to be saying that every time ancient writers used the term *psallo* in a musical sense it involved the playing of an instrument. This is simply not true.

The various senses of *psallo*, including its New Testament connotation of vocal music, have been duly noted in scholarship.[10] Delling writes concerning the several uses of *psallo* in the Greek Old Testament and acknowledges the use of the term in both instrumental and non-instrumental contexts. He concludes, "Hence one must take into account a shift of meaning in the LXX in other passages in which the idea of playing is not evident."[11] He writes further concerning the use of *psallo* in Ephesians 5:19, "The literal sense 'by or with the playing of strings,' still found in the LXX, is now employed figuratively."[12]

Commenting on the use of *psallo* in Romans 15:9, Leon Morris writes, "[*Psallo*] referred originally to plucking the strings of a musical instrument; later it appears to have been used of singing with accompaniment and then simply of singing."[13] And F.F. Bruce writes concerning the terms *psalmos* (psalm) and *psallo* in comments on Colossians 3:16:

> Nor should the etymological force of the terms be pressed, as though [*psalmos*] inevitably meant a song sung to the accompaniment of a stringed instrument (psaltery or lute), the strings of which were plucked by the hand. While such plucking of the strings is the original sense of [*psallo*] (found in the parallel passage in Eph. 5:19), it is used in the NT with the meaning "to sing psalms" (1 Cor. 14:15; Jas. 5:13; so too, probably, in the LXX quotation in Rom. 15:9).[14]

If one wishes to appeal to the etymological root of *psallo* in his argument, he must understand that the root meaning of *psallo* is not "playing a musical instrument or singing to the accompaniment of an instrument." The root meaning of the word is simply "pulling, plucking, twitching," or the like. That which is pulled or plucked has to be determined by the contexts in which the word is used. Sometimes it was the plucking of a bowstring or a carpenter's line; but these objects of the plucking were not in the root meaning of the word. Sometimes the word was used for the plucking of the strings of a lyre; but the plucking of the lyre strings was not the root meaning. The root meaning of plucking was applied to various objects depending on the context in which the term was used. In musical contexts the Greek Old Testament names an instrument to be "plucked," or an instrument that accompanies the singing, when *psallo* is accompanied by a prepositional phrase identifying the instrument, such as in Psalm 144:9, "I will sing a new song to you, O God; on the ten-stringed lyre I will make music (*psallo*) to you." Similarly, in Ephesians 5:19 Paul uses a simple dative construction to identify the instrument that is to be "plucked" or "played" when Christians sing. They sing and make melody "in (on, with) the heart." There is no evidence of a mechanical instrument being used in this passage.[15]

Andrew Lincoln's comments on Ephesians 5:19-20 concisely express how we should understand the apostle's language:

> Although its original meaning involved plucking a stringed instrument, [*psallo*] here means to make music by singing (cf. also 1 Cor 14:15; Jas 5:13), so there is no reference in this verse to instrumental accompaniment .... Believers who are filled with the Spirit delight to sing the praise of Christ, and such praise comes not just from the lips but from the individual's innermost being, from the heart, where the Spirit himself resides.[16]

If one accepts the argument that the command to *psallo* implies the use of a mechanical instrument, as Atchley apparently believes, it seems to me he will have to accept the implication that Christians must sing to such accompaniment in order to obey the command. This is the case whether the instruction is to Christians in corporate assembly or to the individual. If an instrument inheres in the verb *psallo*, then the singing is not being done scripturally when an instrument is not present. Atchley, however, does not believe one has to sing with an instrument in order to please God. He says people can choose to praise God with or without instruments. This concession essentially invalidates the argument that the verb *psallo* inherently means to sing with an instrument.[17]

Atchley may be thinking that the instrument is not required by the term *psallo* but allowed, because one of the meanings listed in some lexicons is "singing with or without an instrument." If this is his contention, it too suffers from methodological imprecision. Moises Silva has pointed out that not only must one not equate the meaning of a word with its history but also not read the various meanings of a word into a specific use.[18] He writes, "Most words in any language have a variety of meanings, but as a rule the context automatically and effectively suppresses all the meanings that are not appropriate, so that the hearers and readers do not even think of them." [19]

None of the contexts of the New Testament passages that speak to music in the worship of the church indicates the presence of mechanical instruments. In fact, the contexts of these passages support the view that they refer to vocal expression. The uniform testimony of church history that the church worshipped without instruments for hundreds of years before they were introduced validates the a cappella understanding of the New Testament texts.

The Law of Exclusion (Argument From Silence)

Atchley says the law of exclusion or the argument from silence is "probably the chief argument" used by people who oppose instrumental music for Christian worship. His formulation of this argument may be summarized as follows: Anything not specifically authorized in scripture is forbidden. Because instrumental music is not specifically authorized, it is forbidden. He then proceeds to point out that both instrumentalists and anti-instrumentalists often do things that are not specifically authorized in Scripture. He further calls attention to a number of issues that have been associated with division in the ranks of the Restoration Movement in which this interpretive principle has been involved.

Before presenting my own perspective about an argument from silence as it relates to instrumental music, I offer some passing observations on Atchley's argument at this point.

- First, it is striking to note that brother Atchley acknowledges that the New Testament is silent on instrumental music in worship. Despite his rigorous efforts to show that New Testament commands to sing psalms, New Testament quotations of messianic prophecies, Jesus' parable of the prodigal son, the presence of Jesus and the early Christians in the temple courts, and the words *zamar* and *psallo* justify instrumental music as Christian praise, Atchley remarkably says the New Testament is silent on instrumental music. Unlike his fellow advocate Milton Jones who says, "the silence is not as deafening as we have always presumed," [20] Atchley recognizes the silence of the New Testament on the instrument.
- Second, Atchley says that silence in the Bible is "neither inherently prescriptive nor prohibitive." Elaborating on his view he says:

> I don't believe just because the Bible is silent you can do whatever you want. I don't believe because the Bible is silent you can't do anything. When the Bible is silent on a question you have to do good theology. You have to read the Bible and gain from it the principles necessary to help you make what you think is the most God honoring decision.

I agree in principle with brother Atchley at this point. The major question to consider is, however, has Atchley's assessment of the data related to this issue been adequate to break the silence? Has he done "good theology?" [21]

- And finally, I would be remiss not to agree that there have been problems associated with the law of exclusion or argument from silence. But the problems have resulted not from the principles themselves but from an inadequate understanding of the principles and a flawed application of them. To the degree that a cappella advocates have formulated the argument as Atchley has formulated it we have contributed to the confusion. However, in the words of Ashby L. Camp who evaluates Milton Jones' attack against the argument from silence, the characterization of these principles is "so simplistic as to be misleading." [22]

Silence in Contexts

The case for a cappella music only and against instrumental music does not rest merely on the fact that the New Testament is silent regarding the instrument. The silence of the New Testament regarding instrumental music becomes significant because of the contexts in which it occurs.

• First, the silence of the New Testament regarding the use of instruments for Christian praise must be assessed in the theological context of Scripture's emphasis that the sacrificial cult of the Old Covenant, of which instrumental music was an integral part, has been superseded by the New Covenant of Jesus Christ. As I mentioned earlier, Atchley thinks people have made too much of this argument, but he does not offer any substantial response to it. Respectfully, I believe Atchley has made too little of a truth that is certainly not peripheral in biblical teaching.

By his own argument Atchley acknowledges that instruments were vehicles of worship under the Old Covenant, and passages he cites show the connection of instruments with the sacrificial ritual that centered in the temple (2 Chronicles 5:12-14; 7:1-7; 29:25-28). New Testament texts point out that the external elements of the Old Covenant worship were only shadows of the realities that have come to fulfillment in Christ (Hebrews 7:1-10:18; Colossians 2:16-17). Of course we understand that not every aspect of Old Covenant worship was eclipsed by the New Covenant of Jesus because some are identified as present in the worship of the church. Prayer and song were common in the Old Covenant worship and were also practiced by the apostolic church with God's approval (1 Corinthians 14:15). However, there is no evidence that incense and instruments that were part of the Old Covenant worship were part of the church's practice.

A reasonable explanation of the presence of song but the absence of instruments is that the former suited the worship of the New Covenant while the latter did not. New Testament texts reveal that the earliest Christians understood the external acts of Old Covenant worship metaphorically. Instead of embracing the physical temple in Jerusalem the church viewed individual Christians (1 Corinthians 6:19) and the corporate church (1 Corinthians 3:16; 2 Corinthians 6:16; Ephesians 2:21-22) as the temple in which God lives. Instead of offering the sacrifices of the temple cult, Christians were to offer their bodies as living sacrifices (Romans 12:1). The fruit of lips that confess God's name, doing good and sharing with others were sacrifices with which God was pleased (Hebrews 13:15-16). Gifts to a missionary were a fragrant offering, an acceptable sacrifice (Philippians 4:18). Paul's evangelistic outreach to the Gentiles was his priestly duty, and the Gentiles who accepted the gospel were "an offering acceptable to God" (Romans 15:16). In an interesting mixing of metaphors, Peter reminded Christians that they individually were the stones that made up the spiritual house in which they, as a holy priesthood, offered spiritual sacrifices acceptable to God through Jesus Christ (1 Peter 2:4-5).

In the second century, Justin Martyr contrasted "true and spiritual praises and thanksgivings" with Old Testament sacrifices.[23] In the fourth century the preference of song to instruments for Christian worship was recognized by Niceta of Remisiana in a treatise on liturgical singing. He wrote:

> It is time to turn to the New Testament to confirm what is said in the Old, and, particularly, to point out that the office of psalmody is not to be considered abolished merely because many other observances of the Old Law have fallen into desuetude. Only the corporal institutions have been rejected, like circumcision, the Sabbath, sacrifices, discrimination in foods. So, too, the trumpets, harps, cymbals and timbrels. For the sound of these we now have a better substitute in the music from the mouths of men. The daily ablutions, the new-moon observances, the careful inspection of leprosy are completely past and gone, along with whatever else was necessary only for a time – as it were, for children. Of course, what was spiritual in the Old Testament, for example, faith, piety, prayer, fasting, patience, chastity, psalm-singing – all this has been increased in the New Testament rather than diminished.[24]

The implications of the transcendence of the new and better covenant for Christian worship continued to be recognized in the Reformation era. John Calvin's frequently cited words are noteworthy:

> I have no doubt that playing upon cymbals, touching the harp and the viol, and all that kind of music, which is frequently

mentioned in the psalms, was part of the education; that is to say the puerile instruction of the law: I speak of the stated service of the temple. ... But when they [Christians] frequent their sacred assemblies, musical instruments would be no more suitable than the burning of incense, the lighting of the lamps, and the restoration of other shadows of the law.[25]

An argument from silence must be carefully formulated and applied, taking into consideration the change in the covenants. Ashby Camp's point is well taken:

It is true that the failure to mention something need not imply its exclusion. However, the question is not whether in the abstract silence about a matter necessarily restrains one's conduct but whether in the context of Scripture the lack of any indication that God desires or accepts worship from Christians in the form of instrumental music should cause one not to use musical instruments.

As noted repeatedly above, Scripture and church history suggest that instrumental music was an integral part of the sacrificial worship of the Jewish temple that was superseded by the higher worship inaugurated by Christ. Whatever one believes about the effect of silence in some other theological context, certainly in this context it means that instruments should not be used in worship; something positive is needed to overturn the scriptural and historical presumption against their use.[26]

There is no positive instruction concerning instrumental praise in the New Testament that should overturn the presumption against the use of instruments for Christian worship.

• Second, one must consider the New Testament's silence on instrumental worship in the context of its positive instruction regarding vocal music. Although the New Testament is silent regarding instruments in Christian worship, it is not silent concerning the nature of the music that is suited to Christian praise of God and exhortation of one another. The positive instruction of the New Testament regarding vocal music makes the silence concerning instruments all the more significant.

Atchley attacks the argument from silence by raising the question, "What great message of God did He ever communicate by saying nothing about it?" In response to quips like this, it has frequently been pointed out that the Bible itself recognizes that one can sometime infer God's disapproval of a matter about which He is silent. One such case is identified by Hebrews 7:12-14 where the writer argues that Jesus could not have served as a priest under the Old Covenant because He was from the tribe of Judah, not the tribe of Levi. In making the point, the writer says, "For it is clear that our Lord descended from Judah, and in regard to that tribe Moses said nothing about priests" (v. 14).

Nowhere in the Old Testament does God speak concerning priests being appointed from the tribe of Judah. The Old Testament is silent in this regard. However, the case does not rest merely on this silence. The fact of the matter is that God did speak concerning the tribe from which priests were to come, namely Levi. So the silence regarding priests from Judah has significance in the context of the positive instruction concerning priests from Levi. It was not the silence alone that excluded priests from Judah; it was God's positive speaking concerning priests from Levi that excluded them.[27]

Again I point out that the New Testament offers positive instruction concerning vocal music for Christian praise and mutual exhortation. There is no evidence in the New Testament for instruments ever being used for these purposes. There is no command to use instruments from an authoritative spokesperson in the New Testament. There is no example of instruments being used by Christians for praise and exhortation. There is no evidence for instruments; there is silence in that respect. There is evidence for singing; this is the positive instruction of the New Testament. Consequently, singing has New Testament authority; the playing of instruments lacks New Testament authority. Instruments are excluded, not merely by the silence of the New Testament, but by the positive instruction in the New Testament to sing.

As we assess the New Testament's positive emphasis on singing we must evaluate it in light of its teaching concerning the nature of Christian worship and mutual exhortation. Singing is a vehicle for expressing the thoughts of one's heart to God. Thoughts of praise and thanksgiving are given expression verbally in song (Colossians 3:16; Ephesians 5:19;

1 Corinthians 14:15-17; Hebrews 13:15), and the praise and thanksgiving that are verbalized to God should be understood by those who hear (1 Corinthians 14:17). Singing is also a vehicle for Christians' speaking to one another (Ephesians 5:19), teaching and admonishing one another (Colossians 3:16), and edifying one another (1 Corinthians 14:15-17). Vocal music can accomplish these expectations in ways that instrumental music cannot. And none of these practices requires instruments in order to accomplish its purposes.

The absence of instruments in the religious gatherings of the early Christians is surprising when the prevalence of instruments in their culture would lead one to expect them to be present. However, when one considers the nature of the early Christian gatherings as focusing on the rational expression of thoughts to God and to one another, the absence of instruments is understandable. The instruments were not there because they had no function.[28]

Ferguson's caveat is important at this point, however. He writes:

> In making this plea for unaccompanied vocal singing in church I should not be understood as saying that just because the singing is unaccompanied it measures up to the standards of Christian worship – as edifying, spiritual, and an appropriate offering of human beings to God. I am simply saying that vocal music is best fitted to express the nature of Christian worship. And this is also the recognition of theorists of church music.[29]

• Third, the silence of the New Testament concerning instruments in the worship of the church must be viewed in a historical context in which the use of instruments of music was alive and well. The use of instruments in pagan and Jewish circles of the New Testament world is well documented.[30] The silence of the New Testament and early Christian literature regarding instruments in church worship is all the more significant when seen in this context. Such silence calls for a reasonable explanation. In this regard, Ferguson has written as follows:

> My observation is that our brethren who support the use of instrumental music in worship have not faced the full force of the historical evidence against their position. The

evidence of church history confirms the reading of the New Testament that is found among the noninstrumental churches of Christ. The historical argument is quite strong against early Christian use of instrumental music in church. What do I mean by a historical argument? If something was present in the New Testament church, there should be some trace of it later in the practice of the church. If it is not to be found in the early centuries after the New Testament, there should be some clear and convincing explanation of why it disappeared or was discontinued. Where the early historical evidence is full – in this case virtually universal, uniform, and unanimous – about the church's practice, there is a strong presumption about apostolic practice and the New Testament teaching. The absence of the instrument in early Christian assemblies (as shown by the extracanonical evidence) creates a negative presumption about its presence in the New Testament. Instrumental music was abundantly available in the religious practices of pagan cults and was brought to consciousness by reading the Old Testament and remembering the temple ritual of the Jews. Where something was available and every assumption would seem to favor Christian adoption of the practice and yet there is complete evidence of the rejection of the practice in the post-apostolic period, there is every reason to look to a deliberate choice made in the apostolic age. A person must have a good explanation in order to think that instruments were authorized in the New Testament but were not used by Christians for many centuries after the New Testament.[31]

As pointed out earlier, Atchley contends that the absence of instruments in early Christian worship that is reflected by the silence regarding instruments in the relevant literature is due to the decision of the early church to be culturally relevant. The problem with Atchley's explanation is that there is simply no evidence to support it. He says this is the missional justification for the RH church's addition of instrumental worship – it is their effort to reach a culture in which instrumental music is so important. It would serve his purpose if he could demonstrate that the early church made the intentional decision to forego instruments in order to reach their culture. However, this is only Atchley's assertion. He provides no evidence to support it. He runs out some theories that have been offered for the non-use of instruments in the primitive church, all of which he collapses into his explanation that they constituted "the culturally appropriate and missionally strategic thing to do to reach their culture." But he never explains how foregoing instruments was missionally strategic for the first Christians.

Contrary to Atchley's criticism, the New Testament's silence regarding musical instruments in worship should not be dismissed, especially when viewed in light of the New Covenant's abrogation of the Old Covenant cult, the positive teaching of the New Testament on how vocal music suits the nature of Christian worship and exhortation, and the historical evidence from the New Testament era and the post-New Testament church.

Conclusion

Non-instrumental churches of Christ have based our practice of church music on a relatively simple foundation. We have followed the positive instruction of the New Testament regarding vocal musical expression and have honored the silence of the New Testament in respect to any other musical act for Christian praise. Without instruction from God in the New Covenant to praise Him with instruments, without evidence that any church founded and nurtured by the apostles ever used instruments, and without a clear implication of any New Testament text that instruments should be used, we have been content to use only our voices in expressing our heartfelt praise of God and in teaching and admonishing one another in song. Recalling the words of G.C. Brewer cited at the beginning of this evaluation, "We do not use instrumental music in worship because there is no authority for it in the New Testament."[1]

Brother Atchley has made arguments that he believes should convince members of churches of Christ that instruments are biblically authorized for Christian worship. I have sought to evaluate fairly his arguments, and I believe I have shown why they are inadequate.

Earlier I called attention to Atchley's opinion that most members of churches of Christ do not have a problem in their hearts with instrumental music, but no one has spoken to their heads. He, of course, has endeavored to speak to our heads.

Here I would caution all of us whether we have a belief in vocal praise only or a belief in both vocal and instrumental praise. We must not allow what we hold in our hearts (emotionally) to control what we think in our heads (rationally). Emotions are powerful; but we must not allow them to be our ultimate authority. Lionel Ruby warns, "Wishes beget beliefs, for 'the wish is father to the thought,' often regardless of the evidence." [2]

It is difficult for any of us to approach the Bible with complete objectivity. We are all a part of what has gone before us, and our hearts are filled with convictions that we have come to in any number of ways. We have been influenced by family, friends, culture, personal preferences and the like. This is all the more reason not to evaluate the teaching of Scripture through the lens of emotions (our hearts) but to allow Scripture first to transform our minds. Then we can believe in our hearts what our minds find to be convincing.

We must not allow the feelings of our hearts on any issue to be so strong that they keep us from recognizing inconsistencies, inaccuracies and negative implications of the arguments we make and of the arguments we are asked to accept. If I were to embrace brother Atchley's view, I would have to accept the factual inaccuracies, the hermeneutical imprecision and the internal inconsistencies that compromise his arguments. I cannot make such concessions. And I appeal to others not to make such concessions.

Long before I ever learned that there was a question concerning instrumental music in church, G.C. Brewer warned, "When people first want a thing and adopt it, and then later begin looking for the scriptural authority for the thing, they cannot be expected to deal honestly with the Scriptures, as a rule. There are exceptions, of course." [3] I hope we will be among the exceptions.

In the beginning of this critique I pointed out that I am not calling into question brother Atchley's pledge of commitment to the Word of God. I have dealt with his arguments. In so doing I have called into question his incorrect use of Scripture in order to prove his point. Neither do I question brother Atchley's love for God nor his passion for reaching the lost. May the love of God compel us all! However, Jesus reminded us that love for the Lord is a matter of both the heart and the mind (Matthew 22:37). To get this out of balance is spiritually fatal. In this critique I have called to the front matters that, if accepted, compromise our minds, and, if propagated, lead others astray.

Readers of this critique will notice that I have frequently cited the works of Everett Ferguson. I have done so, in part, because Atchley thinks Ferguson has offered the best defense of the non-instrumental position. By carrying out this evaluation in conversation with Ferguson, I hope one can see where Atchley's arguments stand when compared to Ferguson's analysis. I have cited him also because of my own respect for his painstaking scrutiny of the evidence that is relevant to this issue, the methodological precision that drives his work, and the non-judgmental spirit with which he presents his case.

In contrast to Atchley who thinks the question of instrumental music is "way too unimportant," Ferguson recognizes, as should we all, that there is something serious at stake in the discussion of instrumental music, something that transcends the issue of the instrument itself. He writes:

> [T]he use of vocal music alone, unaccompanied by instruments, is one point where churches of Christ have the stronger position – biblically, historically, doctrinally and liturgically. ... Instrumental music in itself may not be so important, but what it represents is important, indeed fundamental, to identity. Much more is involved than "house rules" or tradition. The key dividing line is this: does one in the religious life of the church depend on express biblical authorization? This is what those in the Reformed tradition call "the regulative principle." That is the principle that the church, when acting as a church, is authorized to do only what has biblical precedent.[4]

Readers will also notice that I have occasionally called attention to the work of John Price. I have done so as a means of showing that there are people outside of churches of Christ who have espoused the non-instrumental position as a result of thoughtful reflection. On the basis of their study of Scripture and church history, Price, a Reformed Baptist preacher, and his congregation became "convinced that [they] should no longer use any musical instrument in accompanying [their] congregational singing."[5] At the heart of their reason for rejecting instruments is respect for the "regulative principle" to which Ferguson refers. Price writes:

> The New Testament gives no command for musical instrumentation in the worship of the church. Neither do we find even a single example of instruments ever being used in any of the churches. There is not a word mentioned concerning musical instruments' being used in any of the New Testament churches.
>
> The regulative principle of worship remains, and what God has not commanded in the New Testament we have no authority to use. He has not commanded the use of any musical instruments as He did in the days of Moses and David. Therefore, we have no authority to bring them into the worship of His church. The complete silence of the New Testament on musical instruments is a most compelling argument that they are not to exist in the church. Only singing is commanded (1 Cor. 14:15, Eph. 5:19, Col. 3:16).[6]

In the foreword to Price's book, Edward Donnelly, an Irish Reformed Presbyterian, reflects upon initiatives in Reformed churches to add multiple instruments to their worship on the basis of the influence of culture, the need to retain the loyalty of young people, and the use of instruments in the Old Testament. His remarks are passionate and probing:

> How wise is it to introduce such a momentous change on such a slender and dubious basis? The controversies which may well arise will be the responsibility of the innovators. New Testament practice is against it. The majority verdict of the past is against it. The dangers are patent. If, as reformed Christians believe, the words of our praise must

always be primary, how much can instruments add to the singing of those words? Will the trumpets, tambourines and cymbals which the Old Testament requires really enhance our appreciation of what is being sung? How will churches organize the dancing which is an integral element in such passages (Psalm 149:3; 150:4)? Is this a constructive, edifying course to adopt?

I write as one who, for a lifetime, has sung unaccompanied praise to God. It puts us on our mettle, makes us depend on each other, for there is no fallback – singing or silence! And it can be wonderful! No equipment needed, no obtrusion of human talents, no controversy, nothing to distract from the glorious words – just the voices of the redeemed harmoniously worshipping the Lord. It is my prayer that the following pages may persuade more of God's people to experience in Christ this liberating simplicity. "Through him then let us continually offer up a sacrifice of praise to God, that is, the fruit of lips that acknowledge his name" (Heb. 13:15 ESV).[7]

I share such a concern for members of churches of Christ and our congregational leaders. My prayer is that we will persist in our commitment to offering only vocal praise in Christian worship, not in a spirit of self-righteous smugness or carping judgmentalism, but out of a deep respect for what God has taught us to do. And my prayer is that the shepherds of the RH church and overseers of congregations who have followed their lead or who will be encouraged to follow their lead will reconsider their decision to implement in Christian worship a practice for which, in the words of Edward Donnelly, "there is not a shred of scriptural warrant."[8]

Appendix 1

Atchley's Remarks Concerning the Use of *Psallo* in Literature Outside the New Testament

In his evaluation of arguments made by some non-instrumentalists based on the Greek verb *psallo* that appears five times in the New Testament (Romans 15:9; 1 Corinthians 14:15 [twice]; Ephesians 5:19; James 5:13), Rick Atchley appears to react to remarks by M.C. Kurfees. In his assessment of the word *psallo*, Kurfees affirmed that early in its history it meant to play an instrument, but by the time of the New Testament the word had lost all instrumental connotations and meant only making music with the voice.[1] Atchley says, "the bulk of scholarship" disagrees; however, he does not offer any references to current scholarship for his hearers to consider. He proceeds to affirm that in the Greek Old Testament (Septuagint/LXX) and in the ancient writers Josephus, Suetonius, Chrysostom and Gregory of Nyssa, the term is used to mean "to play an instrument" although he cites no specific passage in any of these works.

In the earlier evaluation I have acknowledged the extreme nature of Kurfees' statement and the recognition of his overstatement by a cappella advocates. I have further shown that the acknowledgement of Kurfees' overstatement does not negatively affect the case for non-instrumental Christian worship.[2]

88 • *Music in Worship*

The purpose of this appendix is to evaluate Atchley's allusion to the use of *psallo* in specifically named ancient sources contemporary with and subsequent to New Testament times. He leaves the impression that the use of *psallo* in these sources supports the view that instrumental worship is appropriate for the church.

In response to my inquiry concerning the "bulk of scholarship" to which he refers, brother Atchley suggested that I begin by consulting Tom Burgess, *Documents on Instrumental Music*. On the assumption that Atchley's references to writers/works outside the New Testament that use *psallo* would at least include those identified by Burgess, I will follow the lead of Burgess in this appendix.

• **Suetonius.** Burgess does not include Suetonius amont ancient writers who use the Greek verb *psallo*. This may be because Suetonius was Roman and wrote primarily in Latin. His most noted work, and the only one to have come down to us virtually intact, is his *Lives of the Caesars*, published about A.D. 120.

Latin borrowed the Greek verb *psallo* and some ancient writers use it in the classical Greek sense to "play on the cithara (by plucking with the fingers)." [3] The concordance to the works of Suetonius indicates that he used the term once. Suetonius says the emperor Titus "sang and played the harp agreeably and skillfully," [4] but this is not a reference to church practice.

By the end of the second century, Christian writers use the term in a vocal sense, to "chant (the Davidic psalms)." [5] This suggests that the term in Latin experienced an evolution in usage like *psallo* experienced in Greek. The major issue for this study is not whether the term was ever used with instrumental connotations, but whether it was so used in the context of the church's worship. The lone reference in Suetonius provides no evidence relative to church practice.[6]

• **Josephus.** In the case of Josephus, Burgess cites six references from the *Antiquities of the Jews*. As would be expected from the *Antiquities*, all of these references concern an incident in the history of the Jews.[7] There are references to David's playing the harp for Saul (VI.214), music accompanying the procession in which Uzza touched the ark and was struck dead (VII.80), Elisha's request for a musician (IX.35), music in the temple in the days of Hezekiah (IX.269), music that accompanied the celebrations of the return from captivity (XI.67), and the celebration of a victory in the days of Judas Maccabeus (XII.349).

These passages use *psallo* with instrumental connotations as is characteristic of the classical use of the term that is reflected in other occurrences of the word in Josephus. Everett Ferguson has pointed out that "the classical use of the *psallo* family of words in Josephus is normative."[8] However, one should note that none of the references in Josephus has to do with Christian worship. The major issue in this discussion is the use of *psallo* in the context of Christian worship, not in the contexts that Josephus mentions.

Because Josephus writes about events that are narrated in the Old Testament, it is in order to call attention to the use of *psallo* in the Septuagint, the Greek Old Testament. Burgess does not give explicit attention to the use of *psallo* in the Septuagint although there are occasional allusions to such use in his quotations from various lexicons. Atchley does not cite specific examples.

• **The Septuagint.** The verb *psallo* occurs approximately 55 times in the Greek Old Testament.[9] In nine verses (12 occurrences) the word translates the Hebrew verb *nagan* and refers to the playing of an instrument. In about 40 other instances, the verb *psallo* translates the Hebrew verb *zamar*. In seven of these passages, an instrument is identified by a prepositional phrase indicating that in these cases praise was rendered on the instrument(s) or was accompanied by the instrument(s). Two of these passages refer to instruments in the context but without explicitly saying someone praised on an instrument or sang with an instrument. Such contextual allusions may suggest indirectly that the singing was accompanied. In about 30 of these occurrences, the verb *psallo* is used without any explicit indication of an instrument. It may be that instruments could be assumed to have been used in some of these texts. However, in others it appears that all that is being indicated is the verbal expression of praise. This is underscored by the language of the respective contexts, as in Psalm 9:1-2, "I will praise you, O LORD, with all my heart; I will tell of all your wonders. I will be glad and rejoice in you; I will sing praise (*psallo*) to your name, O Most High." Or again in Psalm 101:1, "I will sing of your love and justice; to you, O LORD, I will sing praise (*psallo*)."

That the word *psallo* is used in these various ways in the Septuagint is recognized by the standard lexicons and by scholars who have investigated the contextual uses of the term. Gerhard Delling notes the instrumental use of *psallo* in the Septuagint, but he also acknowledges that *psallo* is used in some Septuagint passages in which "the idea of playing is not evident," although he thinks that in some places the thought of "to play" could be introduced.[10]

All this shows that *psallo* does have instrumental connotations in some Old Testament passages. However, it does not have such connotations in all Old Testament passages. It is well attested that there was a trajectory from a use of the word referring to playing an instrument to the use of the word referring exclusively to singing. That this trajectory toward a vocal understanding of *psallo* was already in place in the Septuagint is duly noted in the statement by Delling cited above and by the Bauer, Danker, Arndt and Gingrich *A Greek-English Lexicon of the New Testament and Other Early Christian Literature* in comments on the presence of *psallo* in Ephesians 5:19:

> In the LXX [*psallo*] freq. means "sing," whether to the accompaniment of an instrument (Ps 32:2; 97:5 al.) or not, as is usually the case (Ps 7:18; 9:12; 107:4 al.). This focus on singing continued until [*psallo*] in Mod. Gk. means "sing" exclusively; cp. *psaltes*=singer, chanter, w. no ref. to instrumental accompaniment. Although the NT does not voice opposition to instrumental music, in view of Christian resistance to mystery cults, as well as Pharisaic aversion to musical instruments in worship (s. EWerner, art. "Music", IDB 3, 466-69), it is likely that some such sense as *make melody* is best understood in this Eph. pass. Those who favor "play" (e.g. L-S-J-M; A.Souter, Pocket Lexicon, 1920; JMoffatt, trans. 1913) may be relying too much on the earliest mng. of [*psallo*].[11]

Just as in the Septuagint so also in the New Testament, one has to consider the individual contexts in which the term *psallo* is used. The use of *psallo* in the New Testament passages is consistent with the vocal understanding of the term not that involving mechanical instruments. And the term has been so translated by the major English versions.

Atchley refers to two Church Fathers, Chrysostom and Gregory of Nyssa, who he says used *psallo* to mean "to play an instrument."
• **Chrysostom.** Chrysostom lived ca. A.D. 345-407 and was for a time an archbishop in Constantinople. Burgess cites Chrysostom, but not in terms of his use of *psallo*. He quotes from Chrysostom's comments on Ephesians 5:19, "not so much for the meaning of *psallo*, but for the meaning of the phrase 'in the heart.' " [12]

Atchley does not cite a particular reference in the works of Chrysostom. However, whatever passage(s) he might have in mind must be considered in the context of Chrysostom's opposition to instrumental music for Christians. James McKinnon, who has investigated every passage from the Early Church Fathers relating to instrumental music, says that Chrysostom "had more to say about instruments than any other Church Father," and adds, "all remarks about instruments are unequivocally condemnatory." [13]

Chrysostom viewed the instruments of the Old Testament cult as an accommodation by God to the dullness of the Jews. In comments on Psalm 149 he wrote:

> But I would say this, that in olden times they were thus led by these instruments because of the dullness of their understanding and their recent deliverance from idols. Just as God allowed animal sacrifices, so also he let them have these instruments, condescending to help their weakness.[14]

Chrysostom was more modest in his allegorizing of Old Testament liturgy than were some other Church Fathers; however, he interpreted instruments as well as sacrifices metaphorically when applied to Christians, as did the Fathers typically. In commenting on Psalm 146 Chrysostom uses the verb *psallo* and makes clear his understanding of the relevance of the Old Testament instruments for Christian worship.

> David at that time was singing (*psallo*) in the Psalms, and we today with David. He had a kithara of lifeless strings; the church has a kithara arranged of living strings. Our tongues are the strings of our kithara, putting forth a different sound yet a godly harmony. For indeed women and men, old and young, have different voices but they do not differ in the

word of hymnody for the Spirit blends the voice of each and effects one melody in all …

The soul is an excellent musician, and artist; the body is an instrument, holding the place of the kithara and aulos and lyre. … Since it is necessary to pray unceasingly, the instrument is with the artist unceasingly.[15]

Instead of providing evidence in favor of the use of instrumental music in Christian worship, Chrysostom actually points in the opposite direction. His use of *psallo* in the context of his own pervasive opposition to the instrument proves that the word does not inherently mean "to play an instrument," especially when the worship of the church is under consideration.

- **Gregory of Nyssa.** Finally, as in the earlier cases, Atchley cites no specific reference from Gregory of Nyssa, a Christian philosopher from Asia Minor who died around A.D. 394. Burgess refers to him but not in terms of his use of the verb *psallo*. Burgess cites the use of the noun *psalmos* when Gregory writes, "A psalm is singing which is affected with the aid of instrumental music."[16]

Ferguson has investigated every occurrence in the writings of Gregory of Nyssa of words derived from the *psal-* root. He has shown that in the works of Gregory the term *psalmos* is used to refer to the book of Psalms, an individual psalm, or the title of a psalm.[17] He notes that Gregory's usage "follows customary Christian terminology" and that Gregory's definition of psalm, therefore, is "an historical note on the etymology of the word and has no bearing on its meaning in the Bible or on Gregory's own usage or early Christian musical practice."[18] Ferguson notes eight occurrences of *psallo* in the works of Gregory. Four of the references are to the Old Testament Psalms and the other four "make clear the everyday usage of *psallo* by Gregory and Christians for vocal music."[19] Thus, there is no use of *psallo* by Gregory of Nyssa that supports instrumental music for Christian worship.

Ferguson notes the value of his study of Gregory's use of *psalmos* and related language as "a warning against taking isolated quotations from the fathers, especially those of an etymological or 'academic' nature, without reference to the actual word usage of the individual and the practice of the church in his time."[20]

Atchley has made generalizations concerning the term *psallo* and offered them to his hearers as evidence in support of his case for instrumental Christian worship without a critical assessment of the use of the term in the sources he identifies. He has failed to make his hearers aware of the evidence that supports a vocal understanding of the term *psallo* when used in the context of Christian worship. He leads his hearers to think that these ancient sources support the use of instruments in Christian worship when, in fact, they do not.

Appendix 2

Instrumental Music and the Theology of Grace

On a number of occasions in his lessons advocating the use of instrumental music for Christian worship, Rick Atchley refers to the idea of grace as a prime factor in influencing people away from the exclusively a cappella position to a position that embraces instrumental music. He commends the RH church for being "grace oriented." In response to some who have wondered why he remains with churches of Christ in light of his advocacy of instrumental music, Atchley says:

> [The church of Christ] is filled with wonderful people ... who want to do what is right and good, and if they get grace-centered teaching they will respond to it. That's why I stay, so people can be liberated from the slavery that never should have been imposed upon them.

He says only healthy churches can make the kind of changes he is advocating. He regards the RH church as just such a church because they have, among other qualities, "a grace-based theology." He believes churches of Christ across the country are ready for a "revival of grace."

Atchley contrasts his grace-based approach to the issue with his perception of at least some brethren who oppose instrumental music.

He describes the perspective of some individuals who have severely criticized him for his view as follows:

> [T]hey believe a false gospel, a gospel that says "if I don't get every detail right, not just the details that God made clear but the details he didn't make clear, if I don't get inference and silence right, my eternal soul will burn in hell forever."

Over against this perspective Atchley finds encouragement "by the great numbers of people that are wanting to discover grace, wanting to be liberated."

Atchley's charge that Christians of the non-instrumental persuasion do not embrace a theology of grace but believe unless one gets every detail right his soul will burn in hell forever is hyperbolic to say the least. In 1991, David Lipe and Cecil May had to respond repeatedly to charges leveled by Larry James and Bill Swetmon that non-instrumentalists believe one has to get everything right or be lost.[1] May's response is representative:

> It appears to me that brother Swetmon and brother James are not talking about me, and not talking about most of the people in the church that I know, when they describe our position as being one which says that we must be absolutely right about everything and cannot make any kind of mistake and still be saved. I have never said that, and I don't hear a lot of us saying that.[2]

I cannot say that there are no people in churches of Christ who believe that one's present and eternal relationship with God is based on his/her perfect performance. However, if there are, this is certainly a wrong notion. If any of us is just before God, it is not on the basis of our success in keeping all the details perfectly but on the basis of God's grace offered in Jesus and accessed by faith. If any of us is ever saved eternally, it will not be because we keep everything perfectly. We will be saved by God's grace despite our imperfect performance.

However, the question that must be considered in the context of the present discussion is, Do we who have been saved by God's grace have a responsibility to learn what God wants of us and to comply with His will? Consider again remarks by Cecil May in the discussion mentioned earlier:

> Justification is not deemed to be by perfect knowledge, nor is it deemed to be by perfect obedience, by those of us who maintain that we should follow the pattern of things, including worship, that [is] to be found in the New Testament. On the contrary we believe, and I preach, "By grace are you saved through faith; and not of yourselves: it is the gift of God: not of works, lest any man should boast." ...
>
> ... once you have sinned, you have lost the opportunity to be saved by works, because "saved by works" demands *perfect* performance. The *sinner* has to seek justification in some other way. ...
>
> While we can understand that faith does not require perfect performance, surely we can also understand that faith does require a continual effort to learn more of what God would have us to do than we now know, and also requires us to do everything that we find ourselves able to do of what God has commanded us. Even in the doing of that, even the most faithful of us sometimes falls short. ...
>
> If perfection in any area has to be the basis of our salvation, then we are all lost, for none of us knows enough, and none of us does enough. But if it really doesn't make any difference at all whether in our faith we really seek to follow God, to find his will, to do his will, and to teach his will to others, then surely we understand that we are not walking by faith. And if we do not walk by faith, then we do not have the promise of grace.[3]

In argumentation one sometimes encounters a "straw man," the stereotyping of a position in such a manner as to make it an easy target, easy to be "burned up." Certainly this is the case here. Anyone who takes seriously the teaching of the New Testament understands that Christians are saved by God's grace (Ephesians 2:8-10), stand in God's grace (1 Peter 5:12), and will be eternally saved by the grace that will be given when Jesus Christ is revealed (1 Peter 1:13). At the end of the day, it is God's grace that must be sufficient for us (2 Corinthians 12:9). To leave the impression that non-instrumental brethren do not acknowledge this great truth certainly makes the non-instrumental position unattractive.

I perhaps should speak only for myself; however, I have spoken with enough brethren who share my convictions and have read from enough of others to know that the non-instrumental view is not in conflict with salvation by the grace of God. We believe we are saved by God's grace. But we also believe that God's grace calls us to be obedient to Him. And we believe that to be obedient to Him we must praise Him without instruments.

Jack Cottrell has pointed out that salvation by grace does not imply an unbound freedom. He comments on Paul's teaching in Romans 6:1-7:13 as follows:

> How grace affects our relation to law, and the continuing role of the law in the Christian life, are the main questions answered in this section. It is true that grace sets us free from law (not just the Mosaic Law, but all law) in some crucial ways. Mainly it sets us free from law as a way of salvation, something it cannot accomplish anyway. As corollaries grace sets us free from the condemnation of the law, and it frees us from legalistic motives for obedience. But – and here is the main point – it does not release us from our obligation to obey God's laws, in whatever form they are available to us and apply to us. Under grace we are all the more slaves to God and owe to him our complete obedience, with the goal of achieving full personal righteousness and holiness (Romans 6:15-22).[4]

Brother Cottrell does not share my convictions regarding exclusively a cappella worship, so I do not quote him here in support of my conclusion.[5] I do quote him, however, in support of the view that the acceptance of God's grace does not liberate a person to do what she or he desires but brings an obligation to obey God. My advocacy for non-instrumental worship is not my effort to do what pleases me or to justify myself on the basis of perfect knowledge or perfect keeping of God's law. It is my response to God's grace. I happen to believe that God has taught Christians in the New Testament to approach Him musically without instruments. God's grace doesn't lead me to be indifferent toward this responsibility but to be vigilant in doing what I understand God to have asked me to do.

So the primary issue is not a theology of grace versus a theology of works. The fundamental issue is the one identified by brother Atchley himself, "Is it biblical to worship God with instruments?" If I might elaborate a little further, "Is it biblical for people who have been saved by grace to worship God with instruments?" If brother Atchley's arguments are cogent and the use of instruments in Christian worship is biblically justified, then people who have been saved by grace may worship God with instruments. On the other hand, if his arguments lack credibility, then the straightforward teaching of the New Testament that Christians should simply sing and make melody with the heart must be pursued by those who have been saved by grace.

Appendix 3

Instrumental Music and Eternal Judgment

Discussion of religious issues has always been a sensitive matter. People have been able to discuss their differences of viewpoint on many subjects in a relatively dispassionate manner. However, in the case of other subjects, the emotions become exercised. This is particularly the case when an issue involves matters of religious belief and practice. Even in our postmodern culture, when every viewpoint seems to be regarded as equally valid, once a person expresses his conviction that his view is right, many people who disagree quickly accuse him of being judgmental. In such discussions the real issue at stake is frequently obscured by the inflaming of the emotions. Lionel Ruby has observed:

> Strong feelings and emotions, as is well known, make it difficult to think clearly. Prejudice and bias are responsible for distortions in our perception of facts. Wishes beget beliefs, for "the wish is father to the thought," often regardless of the evidence. And it is hard to be consistent in applying the same standards to others as to ourselves.[1]

An unfortunate diversion of the issue by emotional appeal (from both sides of the discussion) is detected in brother Atchley's discussion of the instrumental music issue.

When Atchley describes the perspective of non-instrumentalists, he leaves the impression that they teach that people who use instruments are "going to hell." If and when people opposed to instrumental music express themselves like this, their language immediately inflames the emotions of people who use instrumental music as worship. After all, no one wants to be consigned to hell, particularly by another human being. And by painting non-instrumentalists with this brush, Atchley contributes to the inflammatory rhetoric.

On the other hand, brother Atchey is equally guilty of passing judgment on non-instrumentalists, although indirectly. He believes that brothers who contend for exclusively a cappella worship are guilty of the legalism that Paul the apostle challenges in the letter to the Galatians. In fact, Atchley says he first came to realize he had to speak out on the instrumental music issue when he was preaching a series of sermons based on Galatians. According to Galatians 1:6-9, a person guilty of the perverted gospel of legalism that Paul attacks should be "eternally condemned." So by implication, brother Atchley shares in the judgmental spirit he decries.

Such accusations from either perspective do not advance the healthy discussion of the issue. At another place in his lessons, Atchley affirms a noble approach when he says there should be clear and respectful communication, an absence of name-calling, no impugning of motives. He says correctly, "If your position is so weak that you have to assassinate someone's character to support it, your position needs to be rethought."

In regard to instrumental music in Christian worship, as with any debatable issue of church practice, let's not allow people on either side of the discussion to be sidetracked by wounded emotions due to our judgmental rhetoric. Let's leave the matter of eternal judgment with the "Judge of all the earth" who will "do right" (Genesis 18:25). None of us is the mediator of God's judgment. The Father has entrusted judgment to the Son (John 5:22). God will judge the world in justice, but not by any of us. Rather, He will judge "by the man he has appointed" and validated by "raising him from the dead" (Acts 17:31). That judgment should rest with God and not with us is clearly reflected in Paul's admonition to the Corinthians: "Therefore judge nothing before the appointed time; wait till the Lord comes. He will bring to light what is hidden in darkness and will expose the motives of men's hearts. At that time each will receive his praise from God" (1 Corinthians 4:5). On that day "God will judge men's secrets through Jesus Christ," not through us (Romans 2:16).

Other people should be grateful that they will not have to stand before me in the final judgment. In the spirit of insights gained from a former teacher, if I were the judge, some people would be allowed into heaven who should not be there and others would be excluded who should be welcomed in. God will not make such mistakes. Although we can live in the confidence that God is a righteous judge and that in Christ we do not have to fear His judgment, it is still sobering to contemplate standing before the judgment seat of Christ (Romans 14:10). In the meantime, although not passing judgment on one another, should we not seek to do what we understand pleases the one who will be our judge?

Analogies are not always perfect, but there may be something helpful here. Which of the following approaches from your child would you prefer? "Dad, if I do this particular act will you disinherit me as your son?" Or, "In respect to this particular act, Dad, what do you want me to do?" Upon reflection, I think any parent would prefer the latter. And I suspect that the Heavenly Parent prefers that we approach Him in search of what He wants us to do rather than trying to find the acts for which He will not condemn us.

I recall again the words of G.C. Brewer concerning the discussion of the instrumental music issue:

> It is not a question of who will be damned or who will not be damned. ... It is a question of what the New Testament authorizes us to do in worship and of what it does not authorize us to do. When we obey God's word, we have God's promises – including eternal salvation. When we refuse or fail or fall short in dong God's will, God will judge us. We are told not to judge one another. (Rom. 14:12, 13.) But

we are told that we shall be judged by the word of God, by the gospel, the law of Christ (John 12:48; Rom. 2:16; James 2:12; Rev. 20:11-14.) And both the Old Testament and the New tell us that if we do in our worship that which men command our worship will be in vain. "But in vain do they worship me, teaching as their doctrines the precepts of men" (Isa. 29:13; Matt. 15:9).[2]

Christians who believe that we should approach God in song without instruments do not do so because we fear that God will send us to hell if we play instruments in church. Instead, we approach God without instruments because we are convinced that in His Word He has taught us that such is what He desires. Our preparation for judgment takes a positive direction as we seek to please God. Paul's words are to the point as he describes his own anticipation of appearing before the judgment seat of Christ:

> So we make it our goal to please him, whether we are at home in the body or away from it. For we must all appear before the judgment seat of Christ, that each one may receive what is due him for the things done while in the body, whether good or bad (2 Corinthians 5:9-10).

Endnotes

Introduction

[1] Brother Atchley does not give definition to the "we" who are not defending biblically non-instrumental worship. Perhaps he is referring to himself and the RH church. Although he believes the non-instrumental position is not biblical and even says he cannot defend it biblically, he must acknowledge that there are many members of churches of Christ who believe they can biblically defend the a cappella position.

[2] Mark Henderson, "The Future of Worship at Quail, Part 2," www.quailchurch.com, accessed May 2008.

[3] Ronnie Norman, "Music Matters, Part 1," www.firstcolonychurch.org, accessed September 2008. The announcement concerning the instrumental service that began in February 2009 also appeared on the church's website.

[4] As representative of the shared perspective, I note the following:

Oak Hills Ministerial Staff and Elders, "The Place of Instruments in Corporate Worship" (July 8, 1999).

Milton Jones, *The Other Side of the Keyboard* (Joplin: College Press, 2005).

Rick Atchley, "The Both/And Church," a three-part series presented to the Richland Hills congregation on Dec. 3, 10 and 17, 2006, www.rhchurch.org/pages/the-both-and-church.

Mark Henderson, "The Future of Worship at Quail, Parts 1 and 2," www.quailchurch.com, accessed May 2008; and "The Family of God at Quail Springs and the Instrumental Music Issue," made available to me by Mark Henderson upon request.

Ronnie Norman, "Music Matters, Parts 1 and 2," www.firstcolonychurch.org, accessed September 2008.

5. Rick Atchley and Bob Russell, *Together Again: Restoring Unity in Christ After a Century of Separation* (Abilene: Leafwood and Cincinnati: Standard, 2006).

6. I am indebted to my colleague Dr. Keith Stanglin for pointing me to discussions of the instrumental music issue even earlier, in the late 1600s, among church leaders in the Anglican and Reformed traditions.

7. G.C. Brewer, *A Medley on the Music Question or A Potpourri of Philology* (Nashville: Gospel Advocate, 1948) 5.

8. Everett Ferguson, "Still the Greatest Threat," *Gospel Advocate* (July 2006): 26.

9. Jack P. Lewis, "New Testament Authority for Music in Worship," *The Instrumental Music Issue*, ed. Bill Flatt (Nashville: Gospel Advocate, 1987) 14.

10. **Within Churches of Christ see:**

Everett Ferguson, *A Cappella Music in the Public Worship of the Church*, 3rd ed. (Fort Worth: Star Bible, 1999).

Everett Ferguson, *The Church of Christ: A Biblical Ecclesiology for Today* (Grand Rapids: Eerdmans, 1996) 268-273.

Bill Flatt, ed., *The Instrumental Music Issue* (Nashville: Gospel Advocate, 1987).

Jimmy Jividen, *Worship in Song: A Study in the Practice of Singing in the New Testament With Implications for Contemporary Worship in Song* (Fort Worth: Star Bible, 1987).

Milo Richard Hadwin, "What Kind of Music Does God Want?", *Directions for the Road Ahead: Stability in Change Among Churches of Christ*, eds. Jim Sheerer and Charles L. Williams (Chickasha: Yeomen, 1998) 54-67.

Outside of Churches of Christ see:

John L. Girardeau, *Instrumental Music in the Public Worship of the Church* (Richmond: Whittet & Shepperson, 1888; Havertown: New Covenant, 1983).

John Price, *Old Light on New Worship: Musical Instruments and the Worship of God, A Theological, Historical and Psychological Study* (Avinger: Simpson, 2005).

Brian Schwertley, *Musical Instruments in the Public Worship of God* (Southfield: Reformed Witness, Southfield Reformed Presbyterian Church, 1999).

11 Ferguson, *Church of Christ* 272. Ferguson observes on the basis of evidence compiled by J.W. McKinnon, "The testimony of early Christian literature is expressly to the absence of instruments from the church for approximately the first thousand years of Christian history."

J.W. McKinnon, "The Church Fathers and Musical Instruments," diss., Columbia University, 1965 (Ann Arbor, MI: University Microfilms, 1974).

12 Brewer, *Medley* 12-13. For further elaboration on some of these issues, see Appendices 2 and 3 in this book.

13 N.B. Hardeman, *Boswell-Hardeman Discussion on Instrumental Music in the Worship* (Nashville: Gospel Advocate, 1957) 63-64.

In 1923, Hardeman emphasized this point as follows: "There are many things that are right within themselves and yet wrong when brought into the worship or service of God, be it as an accompaniment or as an integral part thereof. In that class comes the washing of hands, an act harmless per se, but when used in worship to God becomes vain worship. Further, the eating of meat is an innocent act in and of itself, but when put in the service of God is against scriptural authority. In all candor, the playing upon an instrument is a harmless exercise or enjoyment; but when brought into the service of God, because of its lack of heavenly authority, it becomes an act similar to the eating of meat, like the washing of hands, that I fancy the Savior would describe as a vain worship, holding as it does to the doctrine of men rather than following after what God commands."

14 Alan Highers, "Responding to a Defense of Instrumental Music," *Spiritual Sword* 38.3 (April 2007): 13.

15 See also, Jones, *Other Side* 7-8.

This point was made by Jones before Atchley: "People who grew up in Churches of Christ tend to be 'head' people. We must have an intellectual and rational justification for our practices. But something significant has happened recently among many people from my background. They no longer believe in their hearts that instrumental music is wrong. However, they have discovered that it is very difficult for us to change until we not only deal with our hearts but also with our heads. I hope this little book will give some justification for the heads of those who have already changed their hearts."

[16] In this book a number of expressions are employed in reference to the perspectives that are being contrasted. The expressions "a cappella position," "non-instrumental position," and "anti-instrumental position" all refer to the view that only a cappella music is authorized by God for Christian worship and that instruments should not be used. The contrasting view, for which Atchley contends, that instruments are authorized or permitted by God for Christian worship, is designated the "instrumental position."

Further, the expressions "instruments" and "instrumental music" refer to instruments other than the human heart/mind and music played on such instruments. In accord with the expression "make music in your heart" (Ephesians 5:19), the human heart/mind may be viewed as an instrument. Thus music played on the instrument of the heart is acceptable instrumental music. This book, however, concerns the use of what have often been referred to as "mechanical instruments" – instruments that have been crafted by humans.

Chapter 1

[1] All quotations by Rick Atchley, unless otherwise noted, are taken from the DVDs of a three-part series titled "The Both/And Church" presented by Brother Atchley at the Richland Hills Church of Christ on Dec. 3, 10 and 17, 2006.

[2] M.C. Kurfees, ed. *Questions Answered by Lipscomb and Sewell* (Nashville: Gospel Advocate, 1963) 455. David Lipscomb wrote, "Yet it is not clear that instrumental music was introduced among the Jews by direction of God. ... But it was adopted and approved by the prophets and inspired teachers of Judaism; and was used under the sanction of Moses the lawgiver, himself, and so stands approved of God."

Guy N. Woods, *Questions and Answers: Open Forum Freed-Hardeman College Lectures* (Henderson: Freed-Hardeman College, 1976) 26-30. Woods argued more vigorously that instrumental music was introduced into Israel's worship without divine approval.

Adam Clarke, *The Holy Bible ... With a Commentary and Critical Notes*, Vol. 4 (Nashville: Abingdon, n.d.) 684. Outside of churches of Christ one finds this view advanced by Clarke.

[3] Ferguson, *A Cappella Music* 29, 78. See also Ferguson, *Church of Christ* 272-273.

[4] Lewis, "New Testament Authority" 23; Jividen, *Worship in Song* 71-73; Hadwin, "What Kind of Music Does God Want?" 56.

⁵ Goebel Music, "The New Testament Commands Us to Use Old Testament Psalms," *The Spiritual Sword* 10.1 (October 1978): 23. Upon inquiry Atchley informed me he was quoting from a back issue of *The Spiritual Sword*. I located the remark by Music: "God tolerated this as he did David's polygamy and the rebellious Kingdom, but he approved of neither."

Contrast in the same issue:

Tom Eddins, "Instrumental Music Was Used in the Old Testament": 12 – "Perhaps the most important point to note is that instrumental usage was at the commandment of the Lord. This is explicit in scripture."

Also Winston Temple, "Instrumental Music Is an Aid": 15 – quoting with approval Gus Nichols, "Under the old covenant instrumental music was used by God's command (1 Chron. 29:25-30). It was an integral part of the worship."

⁶ Lionel Ruby, *Logic: An Introduction*, 2nd ed. (Chicago: J.P. Lippincott, 1960) 144-145. "We ought to furnish evidence for our beliefs, and this means that we ought to state the evidence as fairly and completely as it is possible to do so. To deliberately select evidence which is favorable to our thesis and to conceal unfavorable evidence is to violate this law. ... 'Special pleading' is the evasion committed by speakers or writers who carelessly or deliberately overlook 'negative' facts."

⁷ Clarke, *Commentary*, Vol. 2 690-91.

Music, "The New Testament Commands Us" 23. The "virulent defender" of the non-instrumental position that Atchley quotes as denying God's approval of instrumental praise in the Old Testament also says, "Even if it could be established that they worshipped with instruments by divine appointment (as with animal sacrifices, incense, etc.), it would have no bearing on Christian worship under the new covenant."

From the other perspective see:

Ferguson, *A Cappella Music* 31-32; *Church of Christ* 272.

Ferguson, "Music in the Assembly" in *Some Contemporary Issues Concerning Worship and the Christian Assembly*, presented for Harding University's Institute for Church and Family, Searcy, AR, Jan. 2001 (originally presented at The Inman Forum, Ohio Valley College, Parkersburg, WV, 1998). "When the sacrificial system of the Old Testament was abolished by the perfect sacrifice of Christ, its accompaniments ceased too – a physical temple and altar, a separate class of priests, burning incense, and other material offerings. It would have taken an express authorization from God to carry over any aspect of the temple ritual into the New Testament. We have that authorization for singing but not for playing on instruments."

[8] Edward Donnelly, "Foreword" in Price, *Old Light on New Worship* 8-9.

[9] This is one of the oldest arguments propounded by instrumental music advocates. See J. Carroll Stark, "Organs in the Church," *The Evangelist* 10.9 (March 4, 1875): 66.

[10] Ralph P. Martin, *Colossians and Philemon*, The New Century Bible Commentary (Grand Rapids: Eerdmans, 1973) 115-116.

Eduard Lohse, *Colossians and Philemon, Hermeneia – A Critical and Historical Commentary on the Bible*, trans., William R. Poehlmann and Robert J. Karris, ed. Helmut Koester (Philadelphia: Fortress, 1971) 151, n. 148.

[11] *The Greek New Testament*, 4th edition, ed. Barbara Aland, et al. (Stuttgart: Deutsche Bibelgesellschaft, 1993) 887-901.

The early church was familiar with the book of Psalms. According to the index of quotations in this edition of *The Greek New Testament*, there are 79 New Testament texts quoting 58 passages from the book of Psalms. The editors also identify over 300 New Testament verses that make allusions to or have verbal parallels with the language of approximately 100 Psalms. The term *psalmos* itself, however, occurs only seven times in the New Testament. Four times the word refers to the Old Testament book by that name or to a passage from Psalms (Luke 20:42; 24:44; Acts 1:20; 13:33). The other three occurrences are in the instructions concerning singing psalms (1 Corinthians 14:26; Ephesians 5:19; Colossians 3:16). No New Testament passage quotes explicitly from Psalm 33, 92 or 150, that Atchley says are among "the very psalms we are commanded in the New Testament to sing" (although there may be verbal similarities to language in Psalms 33 and 92 in some New Testament passages).

[12] Gerhard Delling, "[*humnos, humneo, psallo, psalmos*]," *Theological Dictionary of the New Testament*, ed. Gerhard Friedrich, trans. and ed. Geoffrey W. Bromiley, Vol. VIII (Grand Rapids: Eerdmans, 1972) 498-500.

Carl Holladay, *The First Letter of Paul to the Corinthians*, The Living Word Commentary (Austin: Sweet, 1979) 185.

Richard Oster, *1 Corinthians*, The College Press NIV Commentary (Joplin: College Press, 1995) 333.

[13] Ferguson, *A Cappella Music* 43-75.

Price, *New Light on Old Worship* 67-154.

McKinnon, "The Church Fathers and Musical Instruments" 260-264.

[14] Atchley offers no evidence of any instrumental music in the church of the New Testament era. The only remark offered in support of his view that

New Testament worship was "almost exclusively a cappella" is his observation that we do not know what went on in every church, for example in India or South Africa. Of course, no human being can claim omniscience regarding early church practice. However, to acknowledge this does not justify including in worship practices that we just do not know about. We do not know if the churches in India or South Africa burned incense in worship, but lack of such knowledge does not justify the practice for us. We must submit to the evidence at hand. Ferguson's assessment of the case is more reasonable. "Although it would be bold to say that an instrument was never used by Christians in their public assemblies, I can say that if it was, it was exceptional and unusual." (*A Cappella Music* 53, 58)

[15] Price, *Old Light on New Worship* 198.

[16] This argument, made in the 1940s by several pro-instrumental brothers, F.W. Strong, Homer Strong and O.L. Mankamyer, is pointedly answered by G.C. Brewer in *Medley*, 45-59.

[17] Walter D. Zorn, *Psalms Vol. 2*, The College Press NIV Commentary (Joplin: College Press, 2004) 104-106.

[18] At times a New Testament writer supports a principle of Christian teaching by appealing to the fact that the point at issue was addressed before the law of Moses was given and was not affected adversely by the law (cf. Galatians 3:15-18; Hebrews 7). However, this does not provide a "blank check" for an uninspired interpreter to support any proposed Christian practice by an appeal to an Old Testament instruction given before the law.

[19] W.W. Otey and J.B Briney, *Otey-Briney Debate* (Cincinnati: F.L. Rowe, 1908) 82-83, 101. Briney contended on the basis of Psalm 45:8 in the revised version, "instrumental music is in the Church of Jesus Christ by prophecy."

[20] F.F. Bruce, *The Epistle to the Hebrews*, New International Commentary on the New Testament (Grand Rapids: Eerdmans, 1964) xlvii-lii.

S. Kistemaker, *The Psalm Citations in the Epistle to the Hebrews* (Amsterdam: Van Soest, 1961).

William L. Lane, *Word Biblical Commentary, Vol. 47a: Hebrews 1-8* (Dallas: Word, 1991) cxii-cxxiv.

[21] Chapter and verse numbers in the English Bible differ at times from those in the Hebrew and Greek Bibles. When this occurs, I cite the passage in English with the corresponding Hebrew or Greek citation in brackets as in the present case, Psalm 45:8 [44:9 Grk.].

[22] James Thompson, *The Letter to the Hebrews*, The Living Word Commentary (Austin: Sweet, 1971) 10.

[23] Lane, *Hebrews 1-8* cxviii.

[24] Lane, *Hebrews 1-8* liv.

[25] D.A. Carson, Douglas Moo and Leon Morris, *An Introduction to the New Testament* (Grand Rapids: Zondervan, 1992) 402.

[26] Justin Martyr, *Dialogue With Trypho* 63, in *Writings of Saint Justin Martyr*, trans. Thomas B. Falls, *The Fathers of the Church* (New York: Christian Heritage: 1948) 248.

[27] Franz Delitzsch, *Biblical Commentary on the Psalms*, Vol. II, trans. Francis Bolton (Grand Rapids: Eerdmans, 1959) 85.

Peter C. Craigie, *Psalms 1-50*, Word Biblical Commentary, Vol. 19 (Waco: Word, 1983) 337.

[28] Charles Augustus Briggs and Emilie Grace Briggs, *A Critical and Exegetical Commentary on the Book of Psalms, Vol. 1*. The International Critical Commentary (Edinburgh: T&T Clark, 1906) 388.

Mitchell Dahood, *Psalms I, 1-50*, The Anchor Bible (Garden City: Doubleday, 1965) 274.

[29] In Hebrews 1:5-13 the writer appeals to a collection of Old Testament texts to support his contention that the Son is superior to angels. The passages are Psalm 2:7; 2 Samuel 7:14; Deuteronomy 32:43; Psalms 104:4; 45:6-7; 102:25-27; 110:1. Such chain quotations were common in rabbinical practice where they "were introduced to indicate the strength of the scriptural support for a given theme." (Lane, *Hebrews* 1-8 cxxii.)

[30] Orson Pratt, *The Seer* (Washington, D.C.: Orson Pratt, 1853-54; fac. Salt Lake City: Eugene Wagner, 1960) 159, qtd. in Cky J. Carrigan, "Did Jesus Christ Marry and Father Children?", www.emnr.org/papers/jesusmarry.htm; accessed June 2008.

The extremes to which one can go by approaching Psalm 45 according to Atchley's method should be apparent. One could argue from this psalm, as did Pratt, a Mormon leader of the 19th century, that Jesus had multiple wives. Pratt wrote, "If all the acts of Jesus were written, we no doubt should learn that these beloved women were his wives. Indeed, the Psalmist David prophecies in particular concerning the Wives of the Son of God."

[31] This argument was propounded in 1914 by J.B. Briney in *Instrumental Music in Christian Worship: Being a Review of a Work by M.C. Kurfees Entitled "Instrumental Music in the Worship"* (Cincinnati: Standard, 1914) 73.

[32] **As representative see:**

Leon Morris, *The Epistle to the Romans*, The Pillar New Testament Commentary (Grand Rapids: Eerdmans, 1988) 505 – "The first quotation is from Psalm 18:49, almost exactly as LXX."

Jack Cottrell, *Romans, Vol. 2*, The College Press NIV Commentary (Joplin: College Press, 1998) 430 – "This is a direct quote from Ps 18:49 (LXX 17:50) and 2 Sam 22:50, except for the omission of 'O Lord'."

[33] Ferguson, *Church of Christ* 269.

See the discussion of "The root fallacy" in D.A. Carson, *Exegetical Fallacies* (Grand Rapids: Baker, 1984) 26-32; also James Barr, *The Semantics of Biblical Language* (Oxford: Oxford University Press, 1961) 100-106.

[34] See the discussion of "Unwarranted restriction of the semantic field" in Carson, *Exegetical Fallacies*, 57-62 and the discussions of word meanings in biblical interpretation in Grant Osborne, *The Hermeneutical Spiral: A Comprehensive Guide to Biblical Interpretation* (Downers Grove: InterVarsity, 1991) 69-71, 81-84; William W. Klein, Craig L. Blomberg and Robert L. Hubbard Jr., *Introduction to Biblical Interpretation* (Nashville: Thomas Nelson, 1993) 240-257; and Barr, *Semantics* 107ff.

These important methodological matters have been addressed in the literature produced by individuals of the non-instrumental persuasion in churches of Christ. See J.W. Roberts, "*Psallo* – Its Meaning: A Review – No. 2," *Firm Foundation* 76.14 (April 7, 1959): 216; "The Language Background of the New Testament," *Restoration Quarterly* 5.4 (1961): 193-204; Brewer, *Medley* 84ff.

[35] Francis Brown, S.R. Driver and Charles A. Briggs, *A Hebrew and English Lexicon of the Old Testament* (Oxford: Clarendon, 1907) 274.

[36] Ludwig Koehler and Walter Baumgartner, *The Hebrew and Aramaic Lexicon of the Old Testament*, Vol. 1, rev. Walter Baumgartner and Johann Jakob Stamm, trans. and ed. M.E.J. Richardson (Leiden: Brill, 1994) 273-74.

[37] Brown, Driver and Briggs, *Hebrew and English Lexicon* 392.

Koehler and Baumgartner, *Hebrew and Aramaic Lexicon*, Vol. 2 (Leiden: Brill, 1995) 389.

[38] Walter Bauer, *A Greek-English Lexicon of the New Testament and Other Early Christian Literature*, 3rd ed., trans. William F. Arndt and F. Wilbur Gingrich, rev. and ed. Frederick William Danker (Chicago: University of Chicago Press, 2000) 351. The lexicon (1096) notes that in the Old Testament the verb *psallo* frequently means to sing "whether to the accompaniment of an instrument (Ps 32:2, 97:5 al.) or not, as is usually the

case (Ps 7:18; 9:12; 107:4 al.)." On the significance of parallelism of both *zamar* and *psallo* with terms that refer to vocal expression see Ferguson, *A Cappella Music* 4-7.

[39] Wm. M. Green, "Concern for the Pattern," *Restoration Quarterly* 10.2 (1967): 101.

[40] McKinnon, "The Church Fathers," 1. McKinnon elaborates further, "The two most striking characteristics of the patristic polemic against instruments are its vehemence and its uniformity. ... It is not the vehemence but the uniformity of the Fathers' position which has important implications for the history of music. The patristic attitude was virtually monolithic, even though it was shared by men of diverse temperament and different regional backgrounds, and even though it extended over a span of at least two centuries of accelerated development for the Church. That there were not widespread exceptions to the general position defies historical credibility" (260-261).

Chapter 2

[1] Atchley actually recognizes that teaching beyond that of Jesus in the New Testament is important. He bases a major part of the first lesson in his series on Acts 15 from which he contends that God expects elders to lead their congregation and expects the body to honor their leadership. However, he makes no reference to the teaching of Jesus in this matter. Of course he cannot appeal to the teaching of Jesus because Jesus never mentions elders of churches even once in His teaching. Apparently Atchley thinks, despite Jesus' never addressing the issue of elders, that the teaching of Scripture outside the Gospels concerning elders should be heeded. The fact that Jesus did not address elders' responsibility does not mean that it is a peripheral issue.

[2] Robert Stein, *A Basic Guide to Interpreting the Bible: Playing by the Rules* (Grand Rapids: Baker, 2004) 140-41.

[3] Neil Lightfoot, *Lessons From the Parables* (Grand Rapids: Baker, 1965) 15.

[4] Lightfoot, *Parables* 15. Students of parable interpretation in the 20th and 21st centuries have increasingly recognized the wrongness of the extreme allegorizing (giving each detail of a parable a corresponding spiritual meaning) of the parables that dominated up until the late 19th century. They have acknowledged, however, that some of the parables appear to assume a certain degree of allegory. For example, Jesus interpreted His own parable of the sower (Matthew 13:3-9, 18-23) by giving specific definition to the sower, the seed and the soils.

A correct understanding of the parable of the prodigal son certainly requires a limited allegorical interpretation in which one recognizes the waiting father as representing God, the wasteful son as representing the tax collectors and sinners, and the elder brother as representing the Pharisees and the teachers of the law. However, responsible interpreters resist returning to the pan-allegorizing of the parables. Atchley does not resist the return by his identification of the music in the celebration as a metaphor for church music.

[5] In addition to the possible implication of instrumental music in Luke 15, Jesus explicitly refers to flute players among the mourners for Jairus' daughter (Matthew 9:23), mentions children's games that involved the playing of the flute (11:17), warns against a person's sounding a trumpet when giving his alms (6:2), and says a loud trumpet call will accompany the coming of the Son of Man (24:31). Advocates of a cappella worship have no objections to instruments in comparable settings. None of these passages, however, refers to the use of instruments in the context of Christian worship.

[6] J. Carroll Stark and Joe S. Warlick, *A Debate* (Nashville: Gospel Advocate, n.d.) 49. In 1903, J. Carroll Stark made this argument for instrumental praise in church: "Where has the Son revealed the Father's disapproval of instrumental praise? He himself worshipped with it in the temple; and while it is written, 'He drove out the money changers,' it is nowhere said he drove out the singers, with their harps and trumpets."

[7] See M.O. Wise, "Temple," in *Dictionary of Jesus and the Gospels*, ed. Joel B. Green, Scot McKnight, I. Howard Marshall (Downers Grove: InterVarsity, 1992) 811-817; W.R. Herzog II, "Temple Cleansing," *Dictionary of Jesus and the Gospels* 817-821.

[8] Jack P. Lewis, *The Question of Instrumental Music in Worship* (Searcy: Truth for Today World Mission School, 2008) 27. Lewis has raised caution at this point by observing, "we have no first-century descriptions of temple worship on which to base such an argument, and we do not have evidence that instruments were in use in the temple at this time. The premise makes assumptions based on either the much earlier Old Testament descriptions or the much later rabbinic descriptions."

[9] In the early 20th century, J.B. Briney sought to justify instrumental music for the church on the basis of the fact that early Christians went to the temple (*Otey-Briney Debate* 113-114; *Instrumental Music in Christian Worship* 87-99).

[10] Acts certainly has teaching relevant to our understanding of baptism and the Lord's Supper. However, the teaching of Acts does not stress the incorporation concept related to baptism or the significance of the Lord's Supper as communion.

[11] See J.W. McGarvey, *A Commentary on Acts of Apostles With a Revised Version of the Text*, 6th ed. (Nashville: B.C. Goodpasture, 1961) 49, 258-61; Ben Witherington III, *The Acts of the Apostles: A Socio-Rhetorical Commentary* (Grand Rapids: Eerdmans, 1998) 161-63.

[12] See Richard Oster, *The Acts of the Apostles, Part II: 13:1-28:31*, The Living Word Commentary (Austin: Sweet, 1979) 121-124 for a discussion of the options in explaining Paul's action.

[13] Atchley does not make clear what he is seeking to prove by this argument. The purpose of his lesson is to justify the use of instruments in Christian worship, not to prove or disprove congregational singing. To contend that congregational singing is not authorized in the New Testament does not address the issue of instruments. Lewis calls attention to the antiquity of this argument tracing it back to the Anabaptists of the Reformation era. He also notes its revival among instrumental music advocates in the Restoration Movement who preceded Atchley (Lewis, "New Testament Authority" 55, 59).

The argument is answered by Guy N. Woods, "Is Congregational Singing Required in the Worship of God in the New Testament Church?", *Gospel Advocate* 127 (May 16, 1985): 290, 292, 296; Lewis, "New Testament Authority," 38-42, 49-52; J.W. Roberts, "Is Singing in the 'Worship' Service Demonstrably Scriptural?" *Firm Foundation* 86 (Aug. 26, 1969): 532.

[14] Note the two words used interchangeably by Paul in Ephesians 4:32 and Colossians 3:13 and by Peter in 1 Peter 4:8-10. See further F. Blass and A. Debrunner, *A Greek Grammar of the New Testament and Other Early Christian Literature*, trans. and rev. Robert W. Funk (Chicago: University of Chicago Press, 1961) 150, sec. 287.

[15] Ferguson, *A Cappella Music* 19. For a persuasive argument that Colossians 3:15-16 and Ephesians 5:18-20 refer to congregational activity see Ferguson, "Church Music in Ephesians/Colossians," in *Freed-Hardeman University Lectures 2002* (Henderson: Freed-Hardeman University, 2002) 90-101; also available at www.foracappella.org. See also Lewis, "New Testament Authority" 41-42.

[16] E.K. Simpson and F.F. Bruce, *Commentary on the Epistles to the Ephesians and the Colossians*, New International Commentary on the New Testament (Grand Rapids: Eerdmans, 1957) 283-285.

Others who understand the language of Ephesians 5:19-20 and Colossians 3:16 to reflect the worship of the corporate Christian assembly include:

Ralph P. Martin, *Colossians and Philemon*, New Century Bible Commentary (Grand Rapids: Eerdmans, 1973) 115.

Eduard Lohse, *Colossians and Philemon.* Hermeneia, trans. William R. Poehlmann and Robert J. Karris; ed. Helmut Koester (Philadelphia: Fortress, 1971) 149-153.

Andrew Lincoln, *Word Biblical Commentary*, Vol. 42: Ephesians (Waco: Word, 1990) 345-349.

Additional references in Lewis, "New Testament Authority" 41-42.

[17] Ferguson, *Church of Christ* 268, n. 94.

[18] See Everett Ferguson, "Congregational Singing in the Early Church," a paper delivered at the symposium "Ascending Voice" at Pepperdine University, June 7, 2007, and available at www.foracappella.org.

[19] The word translated "hymn" in the New International Version is the Greek word *psalmos*, "psalm."

[20] Lewis, "New Testament Authority" 55.

[21] Lewis, "New Testament Authority" 55. Lewis has observed in response to this argument as made by instrumental music advocates in Christian churches, "I argued when I first heard the case, and would argue now, that if the position is correct, then the Christian Church people are condemned by their own contention – condemned because they do something in worship which they admit is unauthorized. They do sing, and they consider it worship; they are not merely entertaining themselves. Either congregational singing in worship is authorized or it is presumptive to use it."

See the evaluation of this argument by Alan E. Highers in *The Highers-Blakely Debate on Instrumental Music in Worship* (Denton: Valid, 1988) 189-90. Also Highers, "Responding to a Defense of Instrumental Music" *The Spiritual Sword* 38.3 (April 2007): 24-25.

[22] Ferguson, *A Cappella Music* 7-17.

[23] While Atchley refers to an unnamed campfire singer who brings his guitar to a picnic where singing takes place, other recent instrumental music advocates make the argument by referring to a slate of popular entertainers. They remind us that if one goes to hear Willie Nelson, Amy Grant or Pavorotti sing he would not expect them to "sing only." Or if we watched someone on *American Idol* we would not expect her to "sing only." The same argument was made in the distant past by J.B. Briney in *Instrumental Music in Christian Worship* (Cincinnati: Standard, 1914) 21-22, 39 and O.E. Payne, *Instrumental Music Is Scriptural* (Cincinnati: Standard, 1920) 101.

This argument depends, however, on the examples that are cited. These brothers make their argument by referring to people who typically sing with instrumental accompaniment. However, if instead of going to hear the singers they mention one goes to a concert of the Yale Whiffenpoofs, he would hear them "sing only," for the Whiffenpoofs are an a cappella group. Or if one watched the Republican National Convention on Sept. 4, 2008, and heard Trace Adkins sing the National Anthem, she would have heard him "sing only," because there was no instrumental accompaniment. In instances such as these the term "sing" has no instrumental connections.

In all such cases it is the context in which the singing takes place that determines whether the singing is accompanied or unaccompanied by instruments. In fact, the argument that these brothers are making concerning our use of the word "sing" actually demonstrates the methodological principle at issue in the discussion of singing in the New Testament. The significance of words is determined by the contexts in which they are used. And no church worship context in the New Testament that employs musical terms refers to or even suggests instruments.

[24] Lincoln, *Ephesians* 346.

[25] This is one of the oldest arguments for instrumental music in church. It was made as early as 1908 by J.B. Briney (*Otey-Briney Debate* 47-48); however, the argument preceded Briney.

[26] Stein, *A Basic Guide* 75.

[27] Klein, Blomberg and Hubbard, *Biblical Interpretation* 445.

[28] William Sheppard Smith, *Musical Aspects of the New Testament* (Amsterdam: Uitgeverij W. Ten Have N.V., 1962) 132.

[29] Delling, "[*humnos*], et al." 499.

[30] Price, *Old Light on New Worship* 202.

[31] Schwertley, *Musical Instruments* 80-81.

[32] In the Old Testament, God gifted Bezalel, Oholiab and the craftsmen with the ability to construct the tabernacle, which they did according to the command of the Lord (Exodus 31:1-11; 35:30-36:1). God's acceptance of their work does not justify the church today using skilled craftsmen to build a tabernacle with its accompanying utensils for use in her worship.

[33] Girardeau, *Instrumental Music* 186. The antiquity of this argument for instrumental music in church is recognized in Girardeau's response to it in 1888.

[34] Brother Atchley says that if someone asked him why his congregation sings only a cappella he could not take his Bible and show them. He says that exclusively a cappella worship (the absence of instruments) is a practice he will not open his Bible to defend. I am wondering what he would say to someone who asked him why his congregation does not dance in their

assemblies. Could he take his Bible and show them? Would he open his Bible and defend the absence of dance as an act of church worship?

Chapter 3

1. Girardeau, *Instrumental Music* 182-184. That instrumental music is neither prohibited nor condemned is among the earliest arguments made for instrumental music. Girardeau responded to it in 1888.
2. Ferguson, *A Cappella Music* 40-41.
3. See page 15 in this book.
4. Ferguson, *A Cappella Music* 5.
5. Ferguson, *A Cappella Music* 5.
6. Ferguson, *A Cappella Music* 18.
7. Ferguson, *A Cappella Music* 40.
8. Ferguson, *A Cappella Music* 43.
9. Ferguson, *A Cappella Music* 48.
10. Ferguson, *A Cappella Music* 73.
11. Ferguson, *A Cappella Music* 43.
12. www.rhchurch.org; accessed August 2007.
13. I do not find the article "Does Anything Happen at Baptism?" on the current RH website. However, there are DVD presentations in which brother Atchley expresses sentiments that are consistent with the article.
14. Price, *New Light on Old Worship* 203.

Chapter 4

1. Atchley does not adequately engage other lines of argument that are significant in the case for non-instrumental worship. Any arguments based on the meaning of words and the import of silence must be nuanced in terms of evidence from history and the theological significance of biblical teaching.

    Ferguson, whom Atchley regards as the best defender of the non-instrumental position, spends over half of his *A Cappella Music in the Public Worship of the Church* (43-84) on evidence from history and doctrinal (theological) considerations that are relevant to the discussion. It is unfortunate that Atchley does not engage these arguments that are made by a cappella advocates.

2. One should consult Ferguson, *A Cappella Music*, in which he cites and discusses evidence from Josephus, Chrysostom, Gregory of Nyssa, and

the Septuagint and its bearing upon the non-instrumental understanding of New Testament worship.

For further analysis of Atchley's references to these non-New Testament sources see Appendix 1 of this evaluation, 87-93.

[3] Tom Burgess, *Documents on Instrumental Music* (Portland: Scripture Supply House, 1966). In response to my inquiry concerning the "bulk of scholarship" to which he refers, brother Atchley suggested I begin by consulting Burgess' work. Milton Jones explicitly recommends Burgess' work in *The Other Side*, 10, as does Mark Henderson in the lessons referred to earlier in this book.

Burgess, intentionally responding to Kurfees, cites a number of "early ecclesiastical and contemporaneous writers" that use *psallo* in its classical sense. He contends that the verb in its New Testament use means "to sing with instrumental accompaniment" (14). Burgess' work is a revival of the line of argument made by J. Caroll Stark ["Organ in the Church," *The Evangelist* 10.9 (March 4, 1875): 66], George P. Slade ["*Psallo* and *Psalmos*," *American Christian Review* 21.4 (Jan. 22, 1878): 25], J.B. Briney, *Instrumental Music in Christian Worship: Being a Review of a Work by M.C. Kurfees Entitled "Instrumental Music in the Worship"* (Cincinnati: Standard, 1914), and O.E. Payne, *Instrumental Music in Worship* (Cincinnati: Standard, 1920).

For critical assessments of Burgess' methodology and conclusions see:

J.W. Roberts, "A Review of 'Documents on Instrumental Music' 1-8b," *Firm Foundation* 86 (1969): 708; 727; 743-44; 759, 762; 775, 778; 807; *Firm Foundation* 87 (1970): 7, 13; 23, 27; 39, 44.

Wm. M. Green, "Concern for the Pattern," *Restoration Quarterly* 10.2 (1967): 99-104.

For a review of Payne's work see M.C. Kurfees, *Review of O.E. Payne's Book on* "Psallo" (Nashville: Gospel Advocate, 1937).

[4] M.C. Kurfees, *Instrumental Music in the Worship or the Greek Verb* Psallo *Philologically and Historically Examined* (Nashville: Gospel Advocate, 1975) 44-45.

[5] Ferguson, *A Cappella Music* 7. Ferguson presents the evidence for his conclusion on pages 5-16.

[6] Ferguson, *A Cappella Music* 16-19.

[7] Ferguson, *A Cappella Music* 19-27, 43-75.

[8] Green, "Concern for the Pattern" 99.

9   See pages 32-36 in this book.
10 Delling, "[*humnos*], et al." 489-503.
    See also:
    J.W. Roberts, "*Psallo* – Its Meaning: A Review, Nos. 1-6," *Firm Foundation* 76 (1959): 183, 216, 292, 356, 420-21, 484.
    Charles Heber Roberson, "The Meaning and Use of Psallo (Part I)," *Restoration Quarterly* 6.1 (1962): 19-31.
    Roberson, "The Meaning and Use of *Psallo* (Part II)," *Restoration Quarterly* 6.2 (1962): 57-66.
    Ferguson, *A Cappella Music* 5-27.
11 Delling, "[*humnos*], et al." 493.
12 Delling, "[*humnos*], et al." 499.
13 Morris, *Romans* 505, n. 51.
14 E.K. Simpson and F.F. Bruce, *Commentary on the Epistles to the Ephesians and the Colossians*, New International Commentary on the New Testament (Grand Rapids: Eerdmans, 1957) 284, n. 118.

    In this connection one should also note these observations in the Bauer, Danker, Arndt and Gingrich *Greek-English Lexicon*, 1096 – "Although the NT does not voice opposition to instrumental music, in view of Christian resistance to mystery cults, as well as Pharisaic aversion to musical instruments in worship (s. EWerner, art. 'Music', IDB 3, 466-69), it is likely that some such sense as *make melody* is best understood in this Eph. pass. Those who favor 'play' (e.g. L-S-J-M; ASouter, Pocket Lexicon, 1920; JMoffatt, transl. 1913) may be relying too much on the earliest mng. of [*psallo*]."

15 *Boswell-Hardeman Discussion on Instrumental Music in the Worship* (Nashville: Gospel Advocate, 1957) 43. In his discussion with Ira M. Boswell, N.B. Hardeman stipulated that *psallo* means "to sing to the accompaniment of an instrument." He proceeded to point out, "But the question tonight, and the only one for consideration, is: What, under the New Testament, is the instrument that accompanies the singing? The apostle Paul, in his peerless announcement, settled that once for all. He says we are to sing unto the Lord and 'psallo' with the heart – not with the fingers, not with the plectrum, but with the heart; and, therefore, the heart is the instrument that accompanies the singing."

    M.C. Kurfees, *Review of O.E. Payne's Book on "Psallo"* (Nashville: Gospel Advocate, 1937) 11-18. Kurfees, "What Is Authorized by *Psallo* in Eph. 5:19?", *Gospel Advocate* 65.37 (Sept. 13, 1923): 895. Kurfees conceded that the etymological significance of plucking is found in *psallo*; however, in the New Testament it must be understood metaphorically as plucking the strings of the heart, not those of a literal instrument.

16. Lincoln, *Ephesians* 346.

17. The argument that the term *psallo* and the derived noun *psalmos* imply the use of instruments for Christian worship has long been an enigma for instrumental music advocates. When the argument was made in the late 19th century by J. Caroll Stark ["Organ in the Church," *The Evangelist* 10.9 (March 4, 1875): 66] and George P. Slade [*"Psallo* and *Psalmos,"* *American Christian Review* 21.4 (Jan. 22, 1878): 25], many instrumentalists recognized the implication of the position and did not wish to accept it. Instrumental brothers, like Isaac Errett, editor of the *Christian Standard*, contended that the instrument was a matter of expediency, and they quickly recognized that if the Stark-Slade view was correct, the instrument was a matter of obligation. See a discussion of these perspectives in J.E. Choate and William Woodson, *Sounding Brass and Clanging Cymbals: The History and Significance of Instrumental Music In the Restoration Movement (1827-1968)* (Henderson: Freed-Hardeman University, 1991) 41-48.

    In his book, *Instrumental Music in Worship* (Cincinnati: Standard, 1920), O.E. Payne argued that instruments were required by the New Testament's use of the verb *psallo*. Although many claimed victory for Payne's pro-instrument argument, few were willing to accept that an instrument was required. The circulation of the Payne book was an impetus for the 1923 Ira M. Boswell and N.B. Hardeman discussion on the issue. Ironically, Boswell would not affirm Payne's position. Payne was consistent in his contention; because the instruments were included in the term *psallo*, we must use them. Most instrumentalists were not willing to view the instrument as an obligation, thus neutralizing the Payne position. (Kurfees, *Review* 7-10.)

    In 1966, Tom Burgess published his *Documents on Instrumental Music* in which he contends that the verb *psallo* in the New Testament means "to sing with instrumental accompaniment" (*Documents* 14). Acknowledging the obvious objection that his position implies that instrumental accompaniment is required, Burgess offers the unconvincing rejoinder that New Testament language gives Christians a choice. When we sing "psalms" the instrument is used, but when we sing "hymns" and "spiritual songs" they may be either accompanied or unaccompanied (*Documents* 117). One wonders whose task it is in a congregation to determine when one or the other of these types of songs is being sung.

18. Walter Kaiser and Moises Silva Jr., *An Introduction to Biblical Hermeneutics: The Search for Meaning* (Grand Rapids: Zondervan, 1994), 54-60.

[19] Kaiser and Silva, *An Introduction* 58.

[20] Jones, *The Other Side* 34.

[21] On the recognition that biblical silence in principle is neither prescriptive nor prohibitive, see: Jimmy Jividen, *Worship in Song* 121-138; F. Furman Kearley, "Hermeneutics, Culture and Scripture," in *Directions for the Road Ahead: Stability in Change Among Churches of Christ*, ed. by Jim Sheerer and Charles L. Williams (Chickasha: Yeomen, 1998) 33-40.

[22] Ashby L. Camp, "Review of *The Other Side of the Keyboard*" 8, 10 (http://www.members.cox.net/theoutlet/). See Jones, *The Other Side* 21-24.

[23] *Dialogue With Trypho 11B* in Thomas B. Falls, *The Fathers of the Church* (New York: Christian Heritage, 1948) 330.

[24] *De utilitate hymnorum 9* in Gerald G. Walsh, *The Fathers of the Church*, Vol. 7 (New York: Fathers of the Church, 1949) 71-72.

[25] John Calvin, *Commentary on the Book of Psalms*, Vol. 1, trans. James Anderson (Grand Rapids: Baker, 1981) 539.

[26] Camp, "Review of *The Other Side*" 10. See further Camp, "Music in Christian Worship" (http://www.members.cox.net/theoutlet/).

[27] Atchley makes an argument based on the quotation of Psalm 45:6-7 in Hebrews 1:8-9 (see page 28 in this book). I assume he is familiar with the overall content of Hebrews 1. In Hebrews 1:5 the writer makes an argument to support the important affirmation that Jesus is superior to angels (Hebrews 1:4). His quotation of Psalm 2:7 is utilized in an argument from silence. "For to which of the angels did God ever say, 'You are my Son; today I have become your Father?' " God did speak to His Son in this respect; He did not so speak to an angel. He was silent. Certainly the identity of Jesus as God's Son is a "great message of God," to use Atchley's words. But notice that in making His point God said nothing about an angel being His Son. The principle involved in an argument from silence, when properly executed, has solid biblical support.

[28] For more in-depth discussion of the theological aspects of the issue, see:

Ferguson, *The Church of Christ* 269-273.

Ferguson, *A Cappella Music* 77-84.

Jividen, *Worship in Song* 15-23, 111-120.

[29] Ferguson, *A Cappella Music* 83.

[30] McKinnon, "The Church Fathers and Musical Instruments" 6-110.

[31] Ferguson, "Early Church History and the Music Controversy," in Flatt, ed. *The Instrumental Music Issue* 98-99.

Conclusion

1. Brewer, *Medley* 12.
2. Ruby, *Logic: An Introduction* ix-x.
3. Brewer, *Medley* 99. Note a similar warning from a contemporary writer, Jerry Camery-Hoggett, *Reading the Good Book Well: A Guide to Biblical Interpretation* (Nashville: Abingdon, 2007) 26: "If we come wanting the text to mean some particular thing, what we want it to mean can distort our understanding the way iron distorts the readings of a compass."
4. Ferguson, "Still the Greatest Threat," *Gospel Advocate* (July 2006): 26.
5. Price, *Old Light on New Worship* 16.
6. Price, *Old Light on New Worship* 49.
7. Donnelly, "Foreword," in Price, *Old Light on New Worship* 9.
8. Donnelly, "Foreword," in Price, *Old Light on New Worship* 7.

Appendix 1

1. Kurfees, *Instrumental Music* 44-45.
2. See pages 68-72 in this book.
3. P.G.W. Glare, ed. *Oxford Latin Dictionary* (Oxford: Clarendon, 1982) 1510.
4. *The Deified Titus* 3.2 in *Suetonius*, trans. J.C. Rolfe, vol. 1 of 2 vols., Loeb Classical Library (Cambridge: Harvard University Press/London: William Heinemann Ltd., 1913) 323.
5. Alexander Souter, *A Glossary of Later Latin* (Oxford: Clarendon, 1957) 331.
6. See further Ferguson, *A Cappella Music* 6.
7. Citations are from *Josephus, Jewish Antiquities*, trans. Ralph Marcus. Loeb Classical Library (Cambridge: Harvard University Press/London: William Heinemann Ltd., 1934, 1937, 1943).
8. Ferguson, *A Cappella Music* 14.
9. For a listing of the relevant data see Charles Heber Roberson, "The meaning and use of *Psallo* (Part II)," rev. and ed. Frank Pack and J.W. Roberts, *Restoration Quarterly*, 6.2 (1962): 57-66. Note the oversight of *psallo* in Psalm 18:49.
10. Delling, "[*humnos*], et al." 493-494.
11. Bauer, Danker, Arndt and Gingrich, *A Greek-English Lexicon* 1096.

[12] Burgess, *Documents* 110.
[13] McKinnon, "The Church Fathers" 183.
[14] Cited in Ferguson, *A Cappella Music* 51.
[15] Cited in Ferguson, *A Cappella Music* 52.
[16] Cited in Burgess, *Documents* 38, 58, 83, 113.
[17] Ferguson, "Gregory of Nyssa and *Psalmos*," *Restoration Quarterly* 22.1, 2 (1979): 79. See also Ferguson's expanded study "Words from PSAL – Root in Gregory of Nyssa," in Hubertus R. Drobner and Christoph Klock, eds., *Studien zu Gregor von Nyssa und der christlichen Spatnatike* (Leiden: Brill, 1990) 57-68.
[18] Ferguson, "Gregory of Nyssa" 80.
[19] Ferguson, "Gregory of Nyssa" 82.
[20] Ferguson, "Gregory of Nyssa" 83.

Appendix 2

[1] *Instrumental Music: Faith or Opinion?* Freed-Hardeman University Preachers' and Church Workers' Forum 1991 (Huntsville: Publishing Designs, 1991).
[2] Cecil May, *Faith or Opinion?* 69.
[3] May, *Faith or Opinion?* 19, 21.
[4] Cottrell, *Romans*, Vol. 1 379.
[5] Jack Cottrell, *The Faith Once for All: Bible Doctrine for Today* (Joplin: College Press, 2002) 446-450.

Appendix 3

[1] Ruby, *Logic: An Introduction* ix-x.
[2] Brewer, *Medley* 12-13.